MASTERING PYTHON FOR OPENAI

A Hands-on Guide to Use GPT-3 and Build Powerful AI Applications, Text Generation, and More

By

Mikasa Mizuki

TABLE OF CONTENTS

WHAT IS PYTHON ARTIFICIAL INTELLIGENCE................ 4

INSTALLING PYTHON AND PYCHARM.......................... 7

HOW TO USE PYCHARM.. 13

INTRO AND VARIABLES 18

EXAMPLE CODE... 31

MULTIPLE VALUE VARIABLES 33

EXAMPLE CODE... 54

CONTROL FLOW.. 56

EXAMPLE CODE... 83

FUNCTIONS 87

EXAMPLE CODE... 100

CLASSES AND WRAP UP 102

EXAMPLE CODE... 140

SETTING UP TENSORFLOW.. 142

EXAMPLE CODE... 147

TENSORFLOW INTRODUCTION 149

CONSTANT AND OPERATION NODES 161

EXAMPLE CODE... 175

PLACEHOLDER NODES 177

EXAMPLE CODE... 188

VARIABLE NODES 190

EXAMPLE CODE	198
MAKING A LINEAR REGRESSION MODEL	201
BUILDING A LINEAR REGRESSION MODEL	207
IMAGE RECOGNITION INTRODUCTION	232
EXAMPLE CODE	235
CIFAR 10 PROJECT OVERVIEW	238
IMPORTANT CIFAR PACKAGES	242
DISPLAY IMAGES PYTHON IMAGING LIBRARY	251
RETRIEVING CIFAR 10 DATA	259
PLAYING WITH CIFAR IMAGES	268
BUILDING A MODEL	276
BUILDING TRAINING DATA AND TRAINING MODEL	289
FRAUD DETECTION INTRODUCTION	297
CREDIT CARD PROJECT OVERVIEW	302
INTRODUCING A DATASET	306
BUILDING TRAINING TESTING DATASETS	315
ELIMINATING DATASET BIAS	329
BUILDING COMPUTATIONAL GRAPH	337
BUILDING FUNCTIONS TO CONNECT GRAPH	349
TESTING THE MODEL	361

WHAT IS PYTHON ARTIFICIAL INTELLIGENCE

So what is artificial intelligence? Well when you think of artificial intelligence you think of something we use. You know, a science fiction movie that is about a robot that, like me, has just computers for brains and is doing things that humans do. This is not exactly what artificial intelligence is when it comes to the practicality of it today. Basically what artificial intelligence is a bunch of code that mimics certain tasks when it works is that when it comes to automation most people think of car factories where a robot comes in does a very specific task and that's all of us our official tells and platform is very similar to that except to really narrow situations that make a big hole and that bigger will actually get you day getting results. But for the most part it's not exactly like there is a robot that is interacting with science fiction. So again what artificial intelligence is essentially is science and training models to make predictions on that data. So you get a graph and graph kind of moves you can trace a model to predict the next year or so if you haven't seen a stock market stock and you want to predict when the next or the next predictions or the next day week month that you wouldn't go through all of its past and you would try to figure out which one would work and eventually you might get an answer. Now artificial intelligence isn't in C right now and you've probably heard the news that automation might take away jobs. Reason why it's so powerful is that test flow, which is what a lot of people use, is now available to everyone so anyone can pick something and make it work for that. And a good example that he uses is that there was a cucumber farmer and the trees were small to pick up the bad cucumbers. And it was actually pretty hard for humans to do that. All of those and all that no computer vision like facial recognition or funny was in the project or a picture is something that is really horrible. So you've heard of Thomas cars. Thomas cars like Tesla are trying to make their artificial intelligence work with just cats. Now there's more things to make in a car such as cars and less recognition. But what you want to do is make everything work with just the cameras. So this camera if you put this project here into artificial intelligence you could realize it has a human eye is so good that you can figure out what's happening what you read it is you can figure out if my eyes were closed or I'm smiling or not this is not science fiction or this is and will once again take little pieces of data and overarching what it does is it gives you reliable data. Now of course the state is fallible. Right. Like a storm prediction is actually really tough to do because the stock market wall is not completely random. There is something you can get slightly better than 50 percent. In fact you'll probably see more proxies and great games in the future as there are definitely ones on Wall Street working on this problem right now. But you will be able to get reliable data but not all. And I guess that is going to get more and more exponential. So how do we start off? Well we have to use Python and while there is other ways you can do Cornell for less which recently came out sooner than I thought and was good because as a bunch of wineries like my list that will help them do graphs we think of artificial intelligence UV-A graphs and predictions all those data on a graph and a bunch of little narrow ideas and a little those little situations more over into some data for you. So just keep in mind when you start artificial intelligence that it is not for beginners. It is actually very complicated and there's a lot of math.

INSTALLING PYTHON AND PYCHARM

Now the first step to building and running Python programs is going to be to set up an environment that will allow us to do so easily. There's lots of ways we can go about doing this. And Mac actually provides a built in version of Python which we can then combine with any kind of a text editor and run through the terminal. However we're going to do things differently, we're actually going to download a nice id e called Python which will allow us to build and run our Python projects with ease in one nice interface. Ok so we're going to go and open up a new Windows chrome or whichever browser you're currently using. And I'm just going to search for a charm download. Now I actually already have it. It's going to be the first link. By the way, I actually have Python and the latest versions of Python downloaded. So I'll just walk you through the steps rather than really downloading and installing it myself. So we're going to go ahead and choose the community edition rather than the pro.

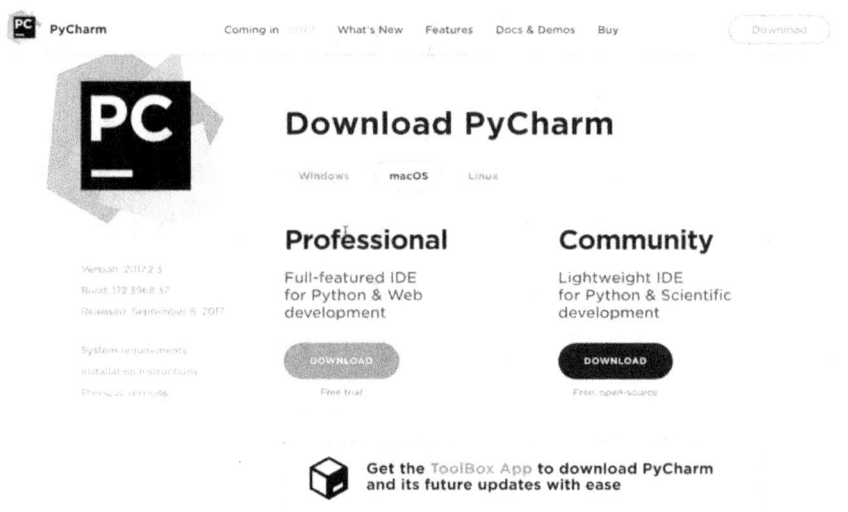

One is pression, one's just a free trial. So go ahead and open up. It's just going to start the download. Like I said I already have the lace version of Prytaneum unlaced version of Python so I'll just show you how to do this. So with the GMG file downloaded which is going to go ahead and open the sky up it's just going to open it and verify it to make sure everything's good and assuming it is we can simply drag and drop it from its current location to our applications folder. I think mindspace to the desktop. So if this window doesn't pop up find out where it's saved and then just drag and drop into applications. Like I said, mine is already there so I'm not going to go through that step again. Once you probably make sure you have the latest version of Python downloaded. So if we go to a Python download K and then select the first link it's just going to provide its ability to download the latest version of Python. Now I think the automatic version is two point seven but I'm going to be using three point six point two because this is going to provide us with all the latest tools. Let's go ahead and download that and just going to take a second. Well again open up this package and now basically this will open up the python installer here. We'll just click Continue continue continue again. Agree with that. Assuming of course you have read it will provide probably the default install location. If you really want to customize things then change your install location by clicking on this but make sure you know exactly where it will install and then we'll just go ahead and click install.

But like I said mine is actually already installed so I'm not going to go through that step. So at this point you probably want to pause the project until you finish installing this should only take a few minutes so I'm going to assume that at this point you have it installed, you have charm installed and you have Python 3.6 point two. So we have all the latest stuff here. So just going to X out of that goes to exile chrome and now we're going to go ahead and open up a new window of pie chart so it should be in your applications there. And again I can actually go ahead and get rid of that so easy Ed. twenty seventeen point two should be the one that we'll be using. And this is just the new project windows so as you can see any previous projects we've done will be on the left here gives us the option to open an existing proto checkout from Version control or just create a new project so I'm going to go ahead and create a new one. We'll have to provide a custom location for this so if you want to choose something differently than click on this and find somewhere to save that I'm going to actually choose a different location here. So you can see and choose a custom location that we want the correct interpreter. And this is why it is important to remember exactly where Python is going to be installed. As you can see versions three point six Make sure you do have that particular version added. Worst case scenario we can actually change this later on but testers do it this step. So with that done we can go ahead and press creates and by the way navigate to your correct

Python version folder as you can see it has two point seven and six options to case. So that will create. And this has just opened up a brand new project for us because this is basically the welcome screen that typically shows some tips you can actually unselect if you don't want to be shown the tips any more. But it's always a good idea to have those tips be displayed. They are usually pretty useful. So with the installation complete add a new window of each arm open. I'm going to end the section here. And coming up right away we're just going to share the idea a little bit. So walk us through what Windows represents or how to create files and how to find the stuff that we need. And just generally get familiar with this particular ID. Like I said, it's really similar to Andrew's studio. It's done by the same people so if you're really familiar with Andrew's studio or even eclipse then you should be quite familiar with this as well.

HOW TO USE PYCHARM

You downloaded and installed PI charm and then used versions of Python correctly so we can go ahead and get started by learning a bit more about the pite charm idea. So let's find the things we need: how to create new python files and stuff like that. So assuming that you just start a new project you hadn't had any existing ones already. This is what your main interface should look like right now. We have this window open on the left and the main window in the center. So this one on the left just represents our project structure. We can open it close up by clicking on this here and basically just provides us a list of all the current files within this particular project. There shouldn't really be any uphaul from our external libraries as we haven't created any yet. Now the possum You may or may not have a window open if you do then you can close it just by clicking on its respective tag here. So we have stuff like the console which would be a way to print messages out as well as take data in. We have the terminal which basically runs like a regular instance of the terminals you would with a Mac.

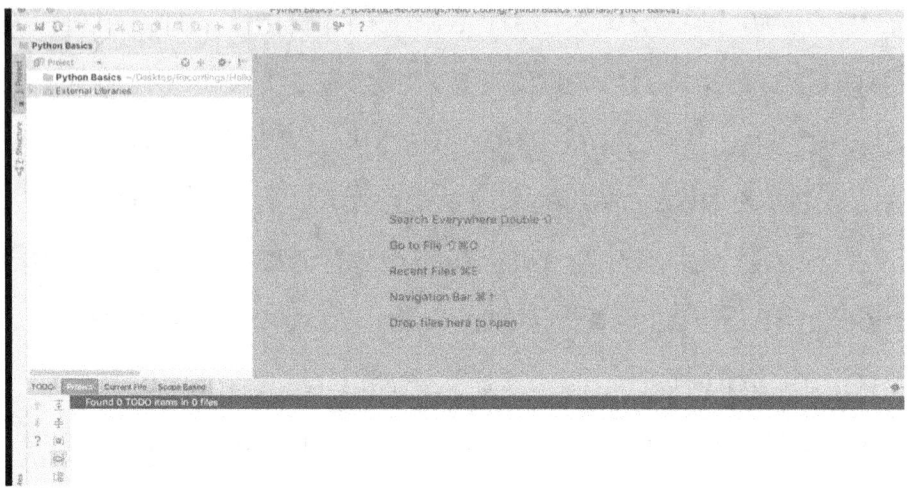

And then we have a to-do list which we haven't don't have any items to do yet. So that's why this is empty. Additionally you can open up this window on the right which provides a date of view but we won't often use that. This has to do with the debugger. Now you can move stuff around if you want. So for example, say ones that display my Python console on the right hand window on the left turn window or on the right hand window I can absolutely move it right into place. So now we can open up my Python console over here. Now I have my menu hidden automatically up top but it's probably going to be visible for you if you don't have it. Also hide. So we're just going to explore this quickly. We click on the Pycroft Community Edition. This has all the information and options that help you customize pajamas shelves so we can go to preferences. We can change stuff like the appearance and behavior when you change edits or stuff itself. How the editor works will often go to our plugins folder here to download and install extra plug-ins and that will give us access to actual frameworks and extra tools as well. We can go to our project here to play from basics and if we open up the project's interpreter we can change a different version of Python we're going to be using by clicking on this. So like I said you do once you generally use the latest version. I'm going to be using three point six point two. So if you're using an earlier version some of the tools that are used may or may not be available to you.

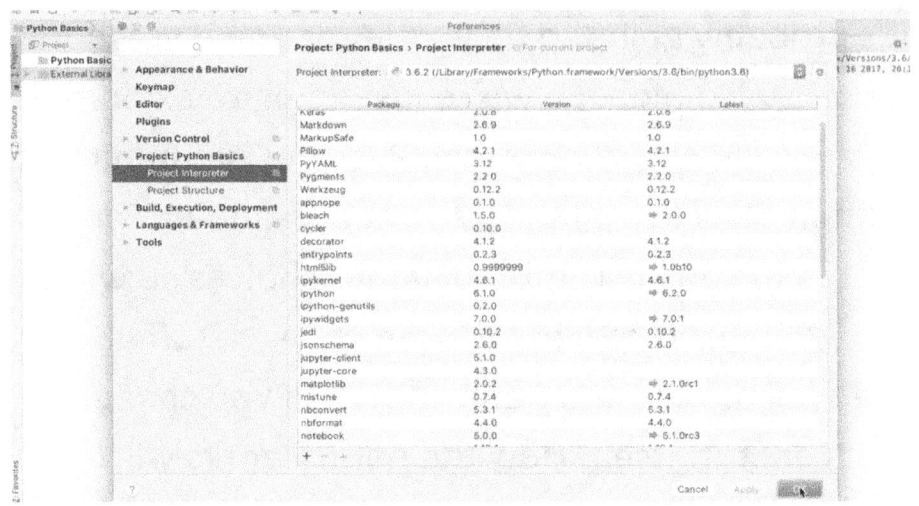

So that's kind of all you need to know from here. We'll click And that's just switch back to this. So as you can see there'll be a variety of menus and these give us access to all the different components of either your project or pie charm or Python itself. Now likely will only be exploring these when we need to open stuff up like for example we need access to the tools we need access to the run configurations and so on and so forth but otherwise give these many testers on yourselves check things out see where things are. Become familiar with your idea. So now we're going to take a quick look at how to create a very simple python program and basically start off by creating a new python file. So we're going to click on our main folder here. Additionally you can go to file new and I'm just going to right click the new file Additionally we can actually choose a python file itself. OK so when we do that both on file and we'll just give this a name we can call this something like new file will click OK and then create a new file to IPY which is the python extension and it tells the compiler that this is going to be a python file not just a regular text file. Alternatively again you could create just a new random file and print a name and then put dot P Y at the end to save it as a python file. Now Python is an extremely flexible and versatile type of language. So realistically if we wanted to print something to the console which is what we are going to do now it would just be as simple as saying something like Prince and then end the quotations. We could say something like Hello. Now if we wanted to run this program what we would do seeing is the run option is not available just yet is to go to all menu. We're going to go to work. I'm going to click on this run. The first one but the second one. And we're just going to choose a new file to be the one that we want to run. So as you can see this will have run our program and will get the run window down here. We could put it up here if we want. And as you can see Hello it gets printed out. All right. So that's really all you need to know to get started. Basically how to create programs on python files and how to run them. Now you can see that this run option is available. Additionally you can go to run and just click on this run here or you can press. You can use this hockey as well. OK so play around with your idea a little bit, get to know it, explore some of these menus, some of the options within them and will start in the next section by learning about our Paice on language basics. So start with just a brief intro and then we'll launch right.

INTRO AND VARIABLES

Now we're going to divide the language basics into our five main sections. The first will be dealing with variables and that's what we're going to cover in this section. So in the variables topics we'll cover First the basic types that we'll be dealing with that we'll take a look at some operations we can perform on numbers and then those that we can perform on strings. Now in this section I'm going to be talking specifically about only single value variables so I'll save stuff like lists, tuples ranges and all that good stuff for the next section as well. I actually just got started in a new file. I called it variables dot PI and it's in addition to my new file here. So any time we go to run this or the very least the first time I go to run it we actually once the code saw Run menu on the search is just clicking on the run here on this run. We actually want to select the second run and then choose our variables files. This is the one we want to run. We no longer want to run your file that contains the stuff that we don't want. So if we go to run this should actually just be basically has nothing printed out here. Now I'm going to move my run up to here so that you can have the two side by side. Now my code on the left and my run window on the right. So I'm going to close up my project. Make sure you have your new file started. And let's begin. So first things first. This is actually a comment and all four of these lines are comments. They are anything that is preceded by this hashtag will the pound symbol is basically going to be ignored by the program nor by the compiler. It's as if it doesn't exist, it's just a kind of test for the code and anyone else is reading the code to read. It's a good place to leave messages and to describe what's happening in the code. Although to be honest we should be writing code that's clear in us that it doesn't really need a description anyway. Actually we can get rid of the file just by closing that and then focus on just variables.

```
# Variables
# Basic types
# Operations on numbers
# Operations on strings
```

So the two main types are categories of variables that we're going to encounter at least single value stuff is going to be numbers. So it capsulizes and then numbers and strings. So numbers obviously represent numerical types. These can be whole numbers or decimals strings or basically anything between our double quotes or single quotes doesn't really Bassal which one we use in Python. And is a good way to represent text or messages within the code. There will be points in time at which we have to distinguish between the two numerical types. So for example integers versus stuff like floats or doubles. But we could essentially treat them as the same for the most part. Now the great thing about Python is that it's what's called weakly types which means we don't have to necessarily assign a specific type to each variable every time we create it. Additionally each variable we create is completely dynamic so we can change its value to something completely different later on in the code as well. No need to declare constants or variables specifically. We can actually just give it a name and a value right off the bat. So for example if I were to create my first number I can just call this number 1 and I can give it the value of let's say 10. I can then later on change my number one as you can see if I go to type out because it's been created already and the variable gives the name. I could actually reassign this to be something completely different. I can give a string value if I want. I can have it contain the value. Hello. And the only problem here which is not really a problem is just a warning it's saying this is not actually used so it's kind of a useless variable. However it doesn't really make much sense to store string value within a variable called number one. So I'm going to call this string one and just have it contain a string value. So this is a numerical value 10. We can actually add decimals on here ten point zero or ten point one of us once and this is the string hello is between the double quotes or Additionally we could put it between single quotes doesn't really matter too much. And again just containing some kind of text or message. So the purpose of some of these calculations we're going to perform. I'm just going to create a number two and I'll set this equal to let's say 7. Now some of the basic operations we can perform on variables include stuff like the following. So we'll have basic addition, subtraction division and multiplication that we can do stuff like the modulus which basically returns the remainder of a division we can perform exponential calculations. And finally we can perform a slower division which basically discards any kind of remainder. Now some of these can actually be performed on strings, namely the addition operator. This can be used to append or stick two strings together. We'll take a look at an example of that in just a second. Now most of these results will just cool on print. So print some kind of results and that is just going to print whatever result we set to the consul over here. So for example if I said just print out my current value office number one and I go ahead and run this now because I set my settings to be running out of variables file here I could just click on the run now and as you can see 10 gets printed out. So let's just go over some really quick examples of some operations we could perform. So let's let Prince number one plus number two. And I'm just going to copy this a bunch of times and seven times. We're going to do it. Number two minus number one or actually number one is the big ones we can do. Number one minus number two to multiply divide. We can raise this to the exponential rate. We'll do it. Modulus was next to the exponential one here. And finally we'll do the division and let's just see what the results of each of these will be. So if we go to run it then as you can see 17 is the addition and subtraction multiplication. This is going to be the division the modulus will basically overturn the remainder. So 10 divided by seven would be one with a remainder of three. That's why we get three printed out. 10 days to the seventh power and then because we're this is going to be the floor division which will basically discard the remainder. 6:50 is one and we throw away that remainder of three. Additionally like I said we can actually concatenate or a pair of strings together. So if I said something like string 1 plus guys OK and then went to run that again. Then as you can see Hello guys gets printed out right there. So every time I recall Prince, unless we do some fancy printing, this is going to print whatever we set these rockets on a new line as you can see in some print tips and tricks right at the very end. Once we finished with all of our language basics but for now this is a very convenient way to print things out and it's totally flexible. Like I said you can put in two variable values like this. You can put in a mix of variable and literal values. This is called a literal string because it's a literal string value. And then we can put in the mix of variables initials or we can actually just how cholesterol's so just print the number 5 and print the number size. So these are the basic numerical operations. Now let's take a look at some string operations we can perform on strings like this. So to help us I'm actually going to take a string too and I'm going to have to say something less complicated. I have to say something like Python is great programming. We'll see if I can spell programming correctly. Programming Language. Now first of all we might want the length of a string so I'm actually just going to comment these all out by the way just use a hot key command and the forward slash slash question mark key will comment everything out and to we can just kind of toggle that comment states so now none of these print statements will be executed and we're just going to move on somehow. Next up down here. So we've already seen we can add strings together or append one string onto the end of another. Again we might want the length of a string so we can actually just Prince lend OK which is going to be short full length and then we can stick a string in here such as we print string one for example this should return the results of 5. We go ahead and run that. And it's because the 5 is going to be printed out right there. Now if we don't want to go up here every time. By the way control all will just automatically run your program so press and control right now you can see that it ran and print cell results. OK so some other operations we might once perform on strings I'm going to put all of these in separate print statements. So if I start typing string 1 or it's during to than just the name of a string dots then I get this list of options to choose from so I can capsulize it if I want. I could do something like string two dots. Find is something that will often do so if I'm trying to find some string within here. Let's see if you can find the string Python in and some other stuff we might want to do just going to put this on a separate line. Again string to dot and then we can scroll through stuff like is. Alpha is decimal. These will tell you obviously if the string is an alpha string so we can do that. And then also do the decimal so it is something like a decimal. Next up we might once to replace items in our string so we could do something like. Again string to dot replace and we can put something like. Great as trying to replace grates with something like. Fantastic. Some other things we might want to do. Print string two dots and then something like splits is a perfectly good one. This will just basically form an array and we'll split out each of the items up based on that say we want to split them based on a space. Every time you find a space it'll create a new item in an array. So let's just go ahead and run these guys. So again a control will run all of them and it will perform the necessary operation. So I appended stuff to it again. This is printing out the number of characters in our string one. Python is a great programming language that just prints this output. Now capsulized So you know that P was capitalized. That was so cool here. It's in the second one after this. This is going to find the word Python. Return the index which starts which indeed is 0 as Python is the first character or the I guess the first substring in this string here. Next is alphanumerics, both returns false as expected. It's now got the string and replaced great with fantastic. And finally the splits based on the spaces are now going to take each of the strings found within this major string and create a new item in an array here.

```python
# Variables
# Basic types
# Operations on numbers
# Operations on strings

# Numbers and strings

number1 = 10
number2 = 7
string1 = "hello"
string2 = "python is a great programming language"

# + - / * % ** //
# print(number1 + number2)
# print(number1 - number2)
# print(number1 * number2)
# print(number1 / number2)
# print(number1 % number2)
# print(number1 ** number2)
# print(number1 // number2)

print(string1 + " guys")
print(len(string1))
print(string2.capitalize())
print(string2.find("python"))
print(string2.isalnum())
print(string2.isdecimal())
print(string2.replace("great","fantastic"))
print(string2.split(" "))
```

```
/Library/Frameworks/Python.framework/Versions/3.6/bin/python3.6 "/Users/owl/De
hello guys
5
Python is a great programming language
0
False
False
python is a fantastic programming language
['python', 'is', 'a', 'great', 'programming', 'language']

Process finished with exit code 0
```

So those are your single value variable basics. Like I said the two major types numbers and strings there are slight partitions again between the numerical types such as floats and doubles and integers or floats and doubles the decimal numbers integers all the whole numbers and then strings again. Anything between the double quotes and the single quotes. Generally we'll be printing out the results of these operations we performed just to get kind of familiar with what we can and can't do with these variables. So I'd recommend you play around with these guys a little bit and trace these operations on some glycerol values and some variable values, see what you can and can't do and get familiar with these two types. Hopefully as you can see already Python is a very flexible language. Seeing as we can pretty easily perform these operations and add things together and stuff like that. So once you are comfortable with both strings and numbers we'll move on to the next section which will be multivalued variables so we'll take a look at stuff like lists ranges and tuples which will again produce a way to store lots of values within a single variable.

EXAMPLE CODE

1. Basic variable assignment:

Python
```
name = "Alice"
age = 30
greeting = f"Hello, my name is {name} and I am {age} years old."

print(greeting)
```
Use code with caution.
This code creates three variables:

name: Stores the string "Alice".
age: Stores the integer 30.

greeting: Uses f-strings (formatted string literals) to create a string with the values of name and age.

2. Different data types:

Python
```
pi = 3.14159  # Float (decimal number)
is_working = True  # Boolean (True or False)

# You can even assign another variable to a variable
favorite_number = age

print(f"Pi is approximately {pi:.4f}")  # Format float to 4 decimal places
print(f"I am working: {is_working}")
print(f"My favorite number is also: {favorite_number}")
```
Use code with caution.

This code shows variables can store different data types:

pi: Stores a floating-point number (decimal) approximation of pi.
is_working: Stores a boolean value (True).
favorite_number: Assigns the value of age (which is 30 in this case).

3. Reassigning variables:

```
Python
# The same variable name can be used to store different values
age = 35
print(f"My new age is: {age}")
```
Use code with caution.
This code demonstrates that you can reassign a new value to an existing variable. Here, the age is changed from 30 to 35.

These are just some basic examples of using variables in Python. As you learn more, you'll encounter more complex variable usage!

MULTIPLE VALUE VARIABLES

Got the hang of these single value variables. Well now we're going to expand on that and talk about multi value variables which is essentially a way to store multiple values within a single variable whereas So far we've only seen one value per variable. There are three main ways to do this in Python. The first is going to be using tuples. Then we can do it using arrays. And finally we can do it using dictionaries as well so each of these three types is very slightly different from the others and has different powers and different usages. And when I say power I mean for example arrays are more powerful than tuples meaning there's just more that we can physically do with them. So go ahead and start a new file that's why I did. I called mine multi value variables and as such because we're going to start a new file we need to go to our run settings when we go to run it's we need to make sure that we are choosing our multi value variables rather than running the previously filled in variables file. So if we just go ahead and run that now we should print a blank screen since we have no print statements on here. And just a few comments. Otherwise let's begin we'll talk about tuples first because they seem to be the most simple out of the three. Now first of all what exactly are two pools. Well like I said tuples are as the theme would dictate one of the ways we can still multiple values within a single variable. Now this is kind of different from arrays and dictionaries which represent essentially lists and maps tuples are just a way to kind of grouped together associated values. So we declare tuples the same way we would any other variable. For example it could say tuples one equals and then some values. But this time we put the values within brackets so we could have just one value. But kind of pointless. We could have two three four five values and so on and so forth however many we want between these brackets. Now this is a tuple full of numbers so if we were to print this one print to pull one and we were to run this is going to mount control all will cause this to run We'll just print out the numbers like this. That basically just prints out all the elements within the tuple. Similar to a numerical tuple which is what we have here. We can have a string to pull So I'm actually going to name these properly called the string tuple. This can just be a tuple with some random strings here. For example we could have like mammoth's we could have a b c and we could have my name Nimish and this would be a perfectly valid tuple. Now I'm just gonna change just to int. Well, let's call this number tuple. It's going to get rid of that print statement similar to both a number and a string to what we can actually have a mix of the two different types so we could have something called a mix tuple and we could set this equal to. Let's say we had a number one. We had some strong laws. And we also had a number. Ten point five. This is also a perfectly valid tuple although Do be careful when we try to perform operations such as finding the maximum or minimum value. We won't be able to in this particular tuple because we cannot compare numbers and strings. Otherwise there are actually a bunch of operations that we can perform on these tuples, for example finding the length of the tuple, finding the maximum or minimum value within a tuple and finding the particular index of an element within a tuple. These are all commonly used to pool operations. A slightly more practical example of a tuple rather than just a bunch of numbers and random strings would be for example in a video game. An inventory item. OK so we'd probably have at the very least an Isom name and a quantity. We might also have something like a price so we could have for example the item name. So I'm actually going to call this item tuple. Ok just trying to use a relational real world example. This might be an ode like a piece of food such as fruits or something. Maybe we have two pieces of fruit and each one is worthless, say $5 or five gold coins or whatever you want to call it. So this would be a valid tuple that we might use in an actual program and name as the string price as quantity as an integer or a number. And then the price also is a number we can even make this a decimal. So when we take a look at some of those operations and actually they're quite easy to cool on these tuples for the most part we call on the operation and then put in the brackets the actual tuple we want to call on. So there's no point printing out all three of these. You know how it's going to go. We'll just print out these or we'll print out the strings or the mix. Let's take a look at some of those operations. Now let's actually just print them and put the operation right within here. So for example the first one might be the Lange's. Now we can get the length of any one of these tuples so I can enter the number to pull or I could enter the length of our string tuple. And if I were to run this would just be printed out 5 and 3 respectively because this one has five elements and my string tuple has only three. Now I can also find stuff like the maximum and minimum So for example the maximum on my let's say the string tuple for example I might want to print this and then I might also want to print the minimum off my number tuple. So keep in mind I actually can't perform these minimax calculations of operations I should say on my item to pull because I have mixed types and we can't compare a string again to a number. Now it's not very clear exactly what's being printed out. So I'm just going to add some additional dialogue. I could do this. I can just add a string and then the variable I want to print so in this case this is just going to be the length of the number tuple here. So it's copy this paste it paste it paste. Obviously I'm going to change. This is now the length of the string tuple. This is the max of the string tuple and this is the man of number 2. So if I give this a save and I've run through. Now these are labeled appropriately so I know exactly what these numbers represent 5 and 3. We know that. Now look at this. The Maxima of the string tuple has kind of found the maximum alphabetically within this tuple. So obviously and is the furthest down the list in our alphabet so that takes on the maximum value whereas the men would be a b c and similar to our numbers. Obviously the minimum is one as is the smallest number in the set. Now lastly we might want to access the particular index of an element within a tuple for some reason. Maybe we want to know what is so that we can call on the tuple name and then get the index. So for example let's say I wanted to find the index of my number three in. Actually let's go with my Isom tuple. Let's say I want the index of my quantities to the index of this number two will. I could print for example the index of elements 2. And then I could just print my sissy Isom to pull dots index. And I simply enter in my element. In this case it is 2 and I'm going to run this again. And as you can see index of element 2 is just the number one. The reason this is the index One is because it indexing starts at zero so this is the zeroth element. This is the first element and the second element. So index 1 is this number two. OK so just some nice common tuple operations. Now again we don't really want to represent lists in which a tuple will typically use arrays or dictionaries because tuples are just a way to group associated values together. So with that being said we can go ahead and comment these commands and the thought slash key which also has a question mark on it will perform a mass comment and let's move to arrays. So arrays actually set up very similarly to tuples. We simply call on the array name equals and then the list of values. This time however we use the square brackets. So a nice example of an array might be something like a grocery list or basically any thing where we need to anytime we need to group together a bunch of values that form kind of a list. So we might call this grocery list. And we just simply set this to a bunch of values within these brackets. I'm going to make this a string array obviously that makes a little more sense to me. And this is going to contain something like eggs. We can have some milk. Maybe we'll have some flour OK maybe Additionally we'll have some busser in here and so on and so forth so we just kind of made a shopping list for some grocery items. OK so we can print this list out just like before we called Prince type in the grocery list to get this around. It's just going to print out everything. Note again the square brackets instead of the round brackets. Now let's say open by the way guys we can actually change a value of these just like we would any other ferryboats I wanted to laserdiscs sign my number to pull to be something else. And it can be completely different. It could then be a mix to pull if I want. Similarly I can change my grocery list to something completely different. So we can now have this be the same thing basically minus maybe you might milk, maybe you no longer need any milk or realize I have some already. So we're going to take that element out. That's fine. I can give this another run through. And as you can see the same list just without milk. So let's say I do not anymore once you access the entire list I just want to access a single element within my list. Well, I'm actually going to get rid of that. I did want my full four elements. So let's say I want my second element. I want this element called milk. I know it's going to be index one. So I just want to print out whatever I can find. So rather than just printing out the entire list I can actually paste it and next to the name of my list. I'm going to put the square brackets and the index of the element I want in this case index one will return the milk. Again I give this a run through and as you can see milk is being printed here. Similarly I can actually access a range of values so let's say I want the first two. OK then the way I format this is the minimum value colon maximum value. Now the minimum value in this case is the first element so I can actually leave this blank if the maximum value is going to be this one. So we have to put the index of the item above the one I once accessed. So this is index 0 index 1. So it's set up a range to be indexed to. So then it stops once he gets to index 2. And if I've run this it should just print out my first two elements eggs and milk. Similarly I can do the reverse and I can maybe Stoss index two and go until the end Cape. And this is going to print on my last two elements if I want for example just my third element. I could call the element index too or I could say for whatever reason two and three. And this is just going to print out my third element flower. So ranges are pretty handy so let's say Now we have a list of items. And we realized that one of the items is actually wrong. I go with my list and I say OK I actually don't need milk anymore but I do need something else I need baking soda perhaps. KATE Well then I might want to replace the settlement with a new element called baking soda so we can create a variable for the pass and a lesser value. And all I need to do is take my grocery list and reassign the elements at index. In this case 1 to be something like again baking soda should work fine. So if I were to print out my grocery list now oops I wanted to copy this issue. Oh there we go. And then Prince again and as you can see my second element is replaced with baking soda. So as simple as accessing the index and then reassigning the value. Similarly I could actually reassign it to something completely different. I could be a sign to a number two or something if I wanted and that's fine. That work just doesn't really make sense in this context. Now let's say I wanted to add items to my list. OK there's a couple of ways we can do this. We can append items onto the end or we can insert items into the middle. And luckily for us both operations are actually quite easy. So let's say first of all I want to just stick an ice mont at the end because that's the easiest thing to do. Let's say Oh no I do actually need Melk. I'm going to stick that back onto the end of my list so we can just say grocery list dots. Append. And inside my brackets here I would put the name of the element I want. I'm just using literal values by the way you can actually create actual variables for these and pass them into the brackets. In this case maybe I do want to add milk again and I just want to print off my grocery list. See the changes occur. So the milk is stuck onto the end there. Now let's say I want to insert something right in the middle of my list so that index to. So index 0 1 and x 2 would push here and shove everything over one. So maybe I realized I need sugar that we're baking a cake or something so I can simply say grocery list dot inserts. And now keep in mind the order in which these arguments need to be passed in so first it once an index then it once the object itself. So we'll add in an index. In this case index to add the objects we want. Is this going to be sugar? So again printing out my new list. Let's take a look at that. And now as you can see sugars inserted where flour was before and everything else is moved up by one. Now we've covered so far creating the list we've covered accessing updating appending and in searching the last operation we might want to perform is to delete the license from the list. And there's again a couple of ways we can do that so we can call grocery list dots removed. And now this is going to take in an object as an argument. So if we know a specific object exists in this case I realized I no longer need a buzzer. Found another part of Baso somewhere then I can simply type in the element Bassa and if it exists within the list we're just going to print out the results as you can see Baso which was the last settlement here is now no longer in existence in this list. Similarly I can do the same thing by calling all my grocery lists. And actually before I do that I can call delete the grocery list and then this time just Palsson an index. So let's say OK to run after reviewing. No longer need baking soda that is indexed 1. So I'm just going to Palsson to reprint my list. And as you can see Baking soda is no longer in our list here. And like above when we got stuff like the length of the tuple and then stuff like the max and min. Absolutely we can do that with a list so it can print my length off the list and then the actual length of the grocery list. Similarly I can do the maximum and minimum max of the list and men for the list. And I'm just going to replace the length operator with loops. This should be the max and then So again just running this is the maximum of my list of sugar makes sense. That's a first in the alphabet and the minimum is eggs again the closest to the beginning of the alphabet. There are a few other list operations we may once perform if we want to check any of them out. Just type in the name of full list dots and then you get this big list of different operations and functions and values that we can retrieve from a specific list. Otherwise there's just one more thing I want to cover with regard to race and that is multi-dimensional arrays so this is essentially a way to store lists within lists or you can think about them as matrices if you want. OK so let's say that I'm creating a master shopping list so I have not only a grocery list but also I have some clothes I need to buy. So I'm going to create my master. I will actually create first this clothes list clothes list and get to set this equal to another array. Maybe I need a T-shirt and some shorts and I need some sunglasses. OK so I only need clothes and groceries. So I'm going to create a master list and append these two lists together. Well not quite append them together. Rather stick them all into one list. So what you can do is create a master list master list or it can maybe be more appropriate would be a shopping list. And I'm going to make this a list of my grocery list and clothes list so the photo then prints a shopping list. And run this then as you can see this is now a list with analysts. First I have my grocery list and then I have my second list. So if we want to access elements within this particular list Wolf we're accessing elements within a shopping list then I'm going to get either my grocery list or close list. So basically each of the elements within a shopping list is itself a list. But if I wanted an element within one of those lists within the list I have to access it by indicating a row and a column. So let's say for example I wanted my short let's go with a T-shirt actually. So this is going to be my second or my second row which is basically the row that adds index one. I'm going to get my first item in the first column so column 0. So I specify this by saying something like a shopping list for row 0. Well actually this is row 1 isn't it. This is the second one. And then I want column 0. So now if I print this as you can see I'm getting the T-shirt back which is exactly what I wanted. So just keep in mind this order It's row first then column and if it helps you think about these lists it's going to be each of the items in the master list is a roll and then within each of those lists those are the columns and the last thing if we want to actually stick this together append list it's as simple as using the plus operator. So now let's say I want to create a master list this time I'm not going to separate it into a list of lists but rather just one big list so I can call this monster list and I can set this equal to clothes list plus shopping not Kro not shopping lists that one plus grocery list and I'm simply going to print off my master list run it and this should print again everything in one big array so it's no longer an array of arrays. It's just all one big array. So there's typical array operations and how to use them again. Practice on your own a bit and will move on to dictionaries. Dictionaries will be fairly short because they're actually similar to arrays and just have a very slightly different prophecy in that each element in the dictionary is a key and value pair. So let's just start by commenting this out OK and let's whoops and let's get to creating some dictionaries. So where and when might we see stuff like dictionaries in code. Well to be honest anytime we have some kind of a mapping between some kind of key and a value that's a good place for a dictionary for example very often in systems you'll have your employees or students or something have some kind of a number. An idea can be employee number, student number etc. and then the name associated with that number because names are not necessarily unique whereas numbers have to be. And this is the whole idea behind dictionaries is that the key is unique but not necessarily the value. So the syntax looks slightly different from a race. We start with the name so I'm going to call this list of students. And instead of the square brackets like this we're actually going to give the curly braces to tell the compiler This is a dictionary and then we're just going to input some key value pairs. So let's say my first key is 0. This is our very first employee and I put the code on and then the value that it takes on. So in this case I'm going to insert my own name. So this is one key value pair the key to the left of the colon. Then the value to the right of the colon and then a comma indicating the next element. OK so in this case my key one corresponds to let's say I have an employee named Jill. Key to my correspondence to someone named Harry and three might respond to might correspond to let's say a Lucy. So just a random list of employees that I might have or a guest list of students in this case and their respective keys. So I guess it's a good place to start just to print these guys out. So if I print my list of students a great list of students get this run. Just going to print out this dictionary here. As you can see, key value pairs are quite clear. Now if I want to access individual elements I actually call upon the key but I get back the value found at that key.

```python
# Arrays
# Dictionaries

# numberTuple = (1,2,3,4,5)
# stringTuple = ("mammoth","abc","nimish")
# itemTuple = ("fruit",2,5.5)
# print("length of number tuple",len(numberTuple))
# print("length of string tuple",len(stringTuple))
# print("max of string tuple",max(stringTuple))
# print("min of number tuple",min(numberTuple))
# print("index of element 2",itemTuple.index(2))

# groceryList = ["eggs","milk","flour","butter"]
# print(groceryList)
# print(groceryList[2:3])
# groceryList[1] = "baking soda"
# print(groceryList)
# groceryList.append("milk")
# print(groceryList)
# groceryList.insert(2,"sugar")
# print(groceryList)
# groceryList.remove("butter")
# print(groceryList)
# del groceryList[1]
# print(groceryList)
# print("length of list is:",len(groceryList))
# print("max of list is:",max(groceryList))
# print("min of list is:",min(groceryList))
#
# clothesList = ["t shirt","shorts","sunglasses"]
# shoppingList = [groceryList,clothesList]
# print(shoppingList)
# print(shoppingList[1][0])
# masterList = clothesList + groceryList
# print(masterList)

listOfStudents = {0:"nimish",1:"jill",2:"harry",3:"lucy"}
print(listOfStudents)
```

```
ultivalue Variables
/Library/Frameworks/Python.framework/Versions/3.6/bin/python3.6 "/Users/owl/Deskt
{0: 'nimish', 1: 'jill', 2: 'harry', 3: 'lucy'}

Process finished with exit code 0
```

So if I wanted to get for example my very first guy. So this is my self I would call upon the key 0. So prints a list of students that have the key zero. This is not index 0. This is the key 0. So if I print that out as you can see I get Nimish back. So let's say I want the value found at the key to keep it just so that the keys correspond with the in the indices. In this case. But that's not always going to be the case. Sometimes your keys might be strings. So if I get the value at the key to then as you can see I get back Harry which is appropriate that's exactly what we should expect. Otherwise we basically access and modify elements the same way so I can say something like lists of students OK at the key three is no longer Lucy. Maybe this is something.

First name that came to mind. So if I run this and that's fine. And now if I print out my list of students I basically replaced Lucy's value or the value found in key three with this value of Tanya. Now the last thing we might want in a dictionary is to print out just the keys or just the values. So I can print out something like a list of students' dot keys. And then similarly I can print my list of students taught values. And this is going to print. Obviously my keys and my values respectively. As you can see I get an array of keys and the array of corresponding values below. OK so that's really the basics of your dictionaries. And with that we conclude our multi value variable section. So they're actually not so difficult to work with, you just have to get used to accessing elements by index and remembering that your index is always going well. I mean unless you use zero indexing counting it's probably going to be one less than you think it is. Otherwise as always I encourage you to play around with these a little bit yourselves. Give these a go try some new values try creating some lists of your own accessing items changing items calling operations on these. So work with tuples, arrays and dictionaries and once you're comfortable with that move on to the next topic which is going to be covering control flow in Python. So take a look at stuff like if statements and we'll take a look at some exciting loops and stuff which will allow us to make decisions about which code we want to execute in our programs.

EXAMPLE CODE

1. Using Lists and Unpacking:

Python
```
# A list can store multiple values in order
fruits = ["apple", "banana", "cherry"]

# Unpack the list into separate variables
first_fruit, second_fruit, third_fruit = fruits

print(f"First fruit: {first_fruit}")
print(f"Second fruit: {second_fruit}")
print(f"Third fruit: {third_fruit}")
```
Use code with caution.
This code demonstrates using a list:

fruits: A list containing the strings "apple", "banana", and "cherry".

Unpacking: The list elements are assigned to individual variables (first_fruit, second_fruit, and third_fruit) in the order they appear in the list.

2. Assigning Multiple Values in One Line:

Python
x, y, z = 10, 20, "thirty"

print(f"x: {x}, y: {y}, z: {z}")
Use code with caution.
This code shows assigning multiple values in one line:

x, y, and z are assigned the values 10, 20, and "thirty" respectively.

Important Note:

Be cautious when assigning multiple variables to mutable objects (like lists or dictionaries) using the second method. This creates references to the same object, not separate copies. Modifying one variable will affect all the others that reference the same object.

CONTROL FLOW

We should be getting fairly familiar with how to use both single and multi value variables so the singles big names and strings multis being tuples of race and dictionaries we covered topics in the previous two sections such as store values and variables how tree values from variables as well as how to modify existing variables values. So we're going to apply all of the stuff we've learned to this new topic which is going to be on control flow. To basically implement some logic within our code. What this will allow us to do is choose which parts of the code we want to execute and when and where we want to execute them based on the outcome of some logical tests. Now as an aside when I say execute I mean run the code it's going to be pretty much the same thing now control so has many forms we're going to be covering just a few of them first if else if and else statements. And then while on for loops but essentially they function more or less under the same pretense. So we're going to test some kind of variable value. This is typically comparing it to another value. For example if I had a variable x and I wanted to see what value it could contain I could write some tests. Is X greater than this value is X less than its value is X equal to this value. And those TESL returns some kind of true or false results based on whether the result is true or false. We can choose to execute code block a or code block b. And those are the basics. If an else and also statements while in full flips are less complex but if we can understand them we'll be able to understand them. This is a really nice concept to understand because once we get to know control flow Lessel Besa is going to allow us to pick and choose again exactly where and when we want to execute certain parts of the code rather than executing every single statement that we write line by line which is what we've been doing so well. So we'll get started in a new file. Unless you want to keep everything in the same file Just be sure to comment out all the old stuff. I called my one control photo pie. Just make sure that when you run this you go to your run menu. Second run window. And you want to choose your new file or you know your same file if that's what you've been working on. So I'm going to choose control flow. It should just give me a blank screen for now. So we're going to start with the simplest form. This is going to be the basic IF statements. And I'm going to use the example of a traffic light weirdly enough. So generally speaking I know I know they're all exceptions but let's keep things simple. Traffic lights have one of three possible states: Barclays either red green or yellow. Now I know that there are lots of other states but let's just assume that's one of these three and let's keep things simpler still. For now let's just assume that a light can either be red or green. So my goal here is to Prince either stop or go depending on what current state my traffic light holds. Now first things first I need some way to represent my current traffic light State and I'll do so using a variable and I'm really going to call this traffic light state. This is going to be a string and going to store the values green within it whereas it could be read. Just choosing green arbitrarily. So the simplest way would be to test to see what value this holds by comparing it to other possible values. Now the first one we might be interested in is to see if my traffic lights state is green OK and if it's green then we want to print something out maybe go out of my traffic let's say it is red. So it's not green then. I'm just going to print out stop with something. OK so let's consider the first case first where we're testing to see if it's green. So the simplest form might be to do something like this in traffic light States. Equals greened. So note the first full if statement to denote the IF statements then this is the test I'm performing to see if the value that this variable currently holds is equal to this string. Out the colon to signify the end of all the tests that I'm going to perform in this block. And then underneath I'm going to press enter. It'll provide the indents and here I'm just going to write the code I want to execute in this case is just going to be printing the word go. Now this indentation is important as soon as we exit out of this indentation we're no longer in this statement. So any code I wrote underneath this is all part of the code that I would execute if this is true. And then if I were to do this and then write small statements here this is stuff that will not be executed as part of the if statement. This is going to be executed after this. This is all garbage code however. So I'm just going to delete that. So basic if statements always follow the same format. If and then the test or tests will show you how to do multiple in one later than the code on signifie the end. The code we once execute if this is true and in this case we don't have an else clause so that's all we really need to do. So now if I were to actually run this script around as you can see go just print it out. But what if my traffic state is red which means that this test fails. Well in this particular case I haven't written the code for the alternative case so nothing happens. So why don't we enter that now. And there's actually a few ways we can go about doing this so I can write an additional If statement to test to see if my traffic light is red. Then I'll do something else. So that's one way of doing things. Chartley state equals red. Then in that case we'll just print stop instead and that's fine. I mean there's nothing particularly wrong with this and if we zoom out and I just ran it it says stop there. However it's a little unnecessary in this case because we know again this is kind of based on assumptions that the traffic stay is either red or green now which means that if it's not green then it's red. If it's not red then it's green. So realistically we only need to perform one test at a time. In this case we're actually performing both tests regardless of the outcome of the previous test. So even if my traffic light is green I still perform the second test because it's part of the difference in statements. So again I can simplify this because I know it's either going to be red or green and just add an ELSE case to this if statements in this case I'm just going to print. Stop. So this is OK for this example because I know that if my traffic stay is not green. So if this test fails then it must be red. So I know it's a prince stop. Similarly if I had these roles reversed and I had stopped if I had read up here. And I was a prince stop and I know it's not red. Then I know it has to be green so I would print go. So as you can see if I were to just go ahead and run this again the same result would be printed because my trust stays green. And similarly if it was red then I guess stop being prince at the not those couple of differences between this format and what we saw previously with the two statements. So the first difference is the fact that this Elle's case is only going to be executed if my first test fails. So this means if my traffic by state is indeed green or if my article I say is red which it was previously this fails. And so this does not get executed therefore I executed this code. But if my traffic I say is green then I'm going to execute this because this is true. So I've run this piece of code and I simply ignore this stuff because this worked out to be true and this is basically saying it's everything above the else cause fails then we'll execute this. You can think about the statement as being kind of like a failsafe. The second difference is the fact that we're actually not testing anything here. The case isn't providing isn't performing any more tests. So most will only ever perform one test in this case. However we know that traffic lights generally have at least three states. So there's going to be a yellow light as well. Well in that case all we have right now the model is just going to print stop but that's not exactly what we want. We want something different, maybe slow down or speed up being printed. So what we have to do is perform an additional test to see now. My Chartley state could be green or yellow or red. If it's not green or yellow then it must be red will Prince stop. So we can do this in a few different ways. I think the simplest way would be just to add an L S which is Shortall else. If my traffic light State equals yellow. Well in this case I'm just going to Prince. Let's be cautious just to slow down for now. So in this particular case we've made stuff a little more complex with first performing this test to see if it's green. If this test fails then we'll perform this test if this test fails then we'll fall back on our else case. Additionally if we wanted to be really safe what we could do is say it's traffic state equals red that will print stop. This would actually be a better way of doing things because if for whatever reason GraphicLy state was something else or maybe there was a typo then we could have the else case be in print something like an unknown action. I don't really know what to do if my traffic stay is for example blue all right so it's generally a good idea to have an ALS case particularly when working with strings because strings are very typo prone which means if we make a typo somewhere and we really needed that string to be exactly the same as some other string then we're not going to get the behavior that we once. So let's test to see what happens with all of all possible values that start off with green and I'm going to zoom out and zoom out there. So we'll go ahead and run this one. As you can see, go is printed out. Now what if this is yellow. What happens then. What we get slowed down Prince that's to be expected. What happens if it's red will stop being printed. And what happens if it's some you know garbage string something that is different from those we get. Unknown actions is exactly the behavior that we loop's behavior that we want which is one to change it back to green. So this statement reads kind of like the following will perform this test first if this test pulses will execute this will print go and then we'll ignore everything else and basically execute any code on any. If this first test fails then we'll move to our second test. If this test passes, execute this and ignore this if this test fails then will move to the third and so on and so forth. And if the third test fails or all of these tests fail then we're going to perform this action which is just going to be Prince unknown action. All right. That's your basic if else if and else statements. But we can still make things more complex. So he mentioned earlier how we might be able to test multiple cases in one single statement. And we can do that through the use of our and then operators. So they look a little like this first hour and the operator looks like this. And now the operation looks like this. So basically and goes between two Tests and signifies that both of them must be true in order for the overall test to pass. I'll explain further in just a second. All again goes between two tests. But in this case only one of the two tests has to pass. The only reason that the test will fail is if both cases on the left and the right hand side fail. So in order to demonstrate these Let's introduce another variable into the equation. And this is going to be something like distance from light. So yellow light is either slowed down or sped up depending on how far away we are from the intersection. If we are right near the intersection really close to it then we might as we'll speed up and keep going through it's actually unsafe to slow down at that point. But if we're quite far from the intersection and cannot safely make it to the intersection in time obviously we'll want to slow down in that particular case. So we need to perform an additional test. And there's a couple of ways we can do this. So first finish the sauce. Let's set the sequel something like 20. And that's right the arbitrary case that if we are all 15 meters or closer so the distance from light is 15 or less then we will speed up and we'll go through the lights. And if it's greater than 15 which is in this case we'll just slow down because we're an unsafe distance away. So I'll show you both ways to do this. First using the and operator. So if my traffic light is yellow and my distance from the lights is less than or equal to 15. Well in this case I actually want to speed up OK because I'm quite close to the intersection. My light is yellow so I'm just going to print speed up instead. But what if my traffic light is yellow and I'm further than 15 meters away. Well now I have to write an additional case in my IF statement here. So I'm just going to copy this and paste it and just put the indentation properly. So now my checklist is yellow and the distance from the light is greater than 15. Well in this case. I want to slow down obviously because it is unsafe. So if I now zoom out and go to test this again I get go. That's green. So let's change my Chatterley state to yellow, run again, slow down and print out here because obviously I'm too far from the lights but if I was 10 meters let's say I get speed up being printed out. So even though the traffic light's state was still yellow because my additional case is different in each of those two examples then I've got a different statement being printed out. So the first Test in this case actually passes because this is true. And this is true. Whereas in this case when this is 20 this is true but because this fails this whole test fails a case of both has to be true for the on to pass. Again this is different from the safer places within or because in this case only one of these two has to be true. If both of them are true, that is still fine. It's only if both of these are false that the overall test fails. So show you actually in my opinion a slightly better way of doing things and that's going to be using nested if statements so I'm just going to copy this and actually comment out and I'm going to change paste it down the bottom and make some minor modifications. So rather than having this and then the and here and adding this extra case I'm actually going to get rid of this. I'm going to get rid of this unavenged create a nested IF statement so this if statement now is actually going to be separate from the case if statements and I'm going to consider this if else if else if an else to be all part of the same statement. So now in this case I'm going to perform an additional test inside of this case so I'm testing for the distance from the light and I'm seeing if it's less than or equal to 15 in this case I'm simply going to print speed up again and I'll do something else. It's all we can do. Else because in that case I know it's safe. I'm going to print slowly so now this is going to accomplish the same task as above. But it's going to be slightly different syntax. So in this case here we had five parts to this statement. Well now we only have four parts. But one of the parts contains additional cases within it. So I think this method is actually less efficient because we have to perform a possible four tests to reach the statement. Whereas here we only have to perform a possible three tests before we reach the else case. And that seems to be the case in all of this nested IF statement is actually more efficient than the ankle's in a lot of cases if there are lots of different possible values that this can hold. Then you probably want to consider the nested IF statement in this case. There's only actually a couple of possible values so it doesn't matter too much. But again we're going to accomplish the same task. So again if this passes we'll ignore everything else. If this fails we'll go on to this test. Now if my charger stays yellow then I need to perform additional tests. So now I'm testing distance from the lights and that's the other case there. And again if this fails then I ignore all of this and move on to my next test. So like I said exact same result it's a pretty slow down is being printed just like in my distance from the light was 10. We should speed up. We do. So that's the basics. If Elspeth and L statements. I do highly encourage you if you're kind of confused about trying some different examples and create some variables, compare the valleys and write some if else if and else statements to Tessie's particular use of nested if statements. Use you and new operators because it's important that you understand these moving forwards. I can't unfortunately right now tell you which times are going to be best for you and which times are going to be best for you nested IF statements. That really comes down to the individual case and what you're trying to accomplish with the if statement overall.

```python
# Control flow
# if, else, elif
# while and for loops

trafficLightState = "yellow"
distanceFromLight = 10

# if trafficLightState == "green":
#     print("go")
# elif trafficLightState == "yellow" and distanceFromLight <= 15:
#     print("speed up")
# elif trafficLightState == "yellow" and distanceFromLight > 15:
#     print("slow down")
# elif trafficLightState == "red":
#     print("stop")
# else:
#     print("unknown action")

if trafficLightState == "green":
    print("go")
elif trafficLightState == "yellow":
    if distanceFromLight <= 15:
        print("speed up")
    else:
        print("slow down")
elif trafficLightState == "red":
    print("stop")
else:
    print("unknown action")
```

But without being said I'm going to assume that you guys are previously comfortable with everything so far. And so we can move forwards to talk about loops. So first of all what are loops because they're actually a little bit different from our else and AI statements while loop is essentially a way to execute multiple lines of code or a line of code multiple times. Even though we might only actually write the code once. OK so this comes in particularly handy when we're dealing with doing the same repetitive task. Lots and lots of times particularly when using stuff like arrays. They have really good loops with arrays because it's a nice easy way to iterate over every element within an array. We'll get some loops and arrays in a little bit. Let's first talk about just a basic while loop because arrays and loops go really well together. So a while loop actually starts off looking a lot like it is statements. But instead of only executing the code inside once an X is saying we're going to execute the code over and over again until the test fails. OK so let's consider this example might be a bit silly but perhaps we have some kind of an endpoint. We have a starting point and we're trying to see how far it is to get to that point. Now the simplest way obviously would be to get the end value of the stock value and just subtract them and that would give you the number of steps you have to take to get from point A to Point B. But let's assume that we wanted to actually print out our progress as we go. And besides there might be other obstacles in the way that might be my has to backtrack or something. So it's not always apparent exactly how many steps we need to take. So what we'll do is start out with an endpoint variable that calls this and points. This is just going to equal 10 or something. Okay. We should have a starting point here. Let's just make the sequel to 3 arbitrarily. And our goal here again is to reach from start point to end point and again print out our progress as we go. Now honestly we could change our point in this particular example. Let's assume that stock appointments and points are fixed and we don't want to change our values. So what we want is something like the current position and we're just going to start by Cessna's equal to the starting point so composition now has the value of the start point. So the simplest way to do this would be to add in a while loop so we'll start by typing while and then we want to put the condition that will test after this. So in this case we'll keep going until we reach our endpoint. So while the current position is less than Iowa and points okay then we're going to execute some code in this case. We will simply increase the current position by once a current position plus equals one. So not how this looks actually almost exactly like an if statement but is different in its execution because we're basically executing this over and over and over again until this fails. That's different from the statement because in the statement we execute we perform this test we execute the code and that's it we're done. So now what we want to do is actually print out our value of current position as we go. Current position Actually no we don't want that in quotations. Not sure I was doing that. And I guess we can print our start current position just to let you know just to solidify the points here. So now I would have run this. Now how do we get all these numbers being preinstalled. I started at three four five six seven eight nine and finally finished up at 10 because of our position here. So clearly these statements have been executed multiple different times as compositions value is changing every time and is being printed out every time. Specifically this loop has run seven times with the first position being the initial value so that one doesn't count. So the way this works is we start out with this test and we say OK current position is indeed less than ten points because right now it's only three. So we'll execute this code to increase it by 1 and we'll print its value. And that's the first iteration done now because this is a while loop. We need to go back up to the top and we need to test this again k composition is now 4. It's still less than Nonpoint so we'll execute this code. Now composition is five, still less than ten points than six and seven and eight and nine. Finally composition will be 10 because we've increased it by 1. So then when we go to form tests we say cake composition is 10 and point is 10 10 is obviously not less than 10. So we can fail this test. And so we can skip over this an extra hour a while loop and then execute any code down here which doesn't exist. But you know if that was code we'd execute it. So it does the basics of the while loop again very similar to an IF statement. It's just you executed it basically over and over again until this test fails. Now that being said, if this test never fails then you get stuck in an infinite loop and that's very bad because obviously that's going to cause your program to crash and to fail. So when designing while loops you always want to make sure that there is some way to exit out of the loop and at some point this test will fail. That being said, this test could also fail right off the bat. If for whatever reason our start point was that like 11 or 12 then we actually get no Loopt execute and no loop iterations. So although they might sound scary and complex loops are actually not so difficult. It's just a way to execute the code over and over again until this test fails. But that's your basic while loop. Now we're going to get into four loops and like I said four loops couple really well with arrays. So why don't we use that example. So I'm just going to create a simple number array here and just call this number array. And it's just going to be a list of a bunch of numbers and you get to answer and some random values here nine Okay that's good enough. These are just completely arbitrary values. So my goal here is now to go through this array and double each of these and then print out the doubled value. A simple enough task that we could actually accomplish just without the use of any kind of loop. We could then say something like the Prince Nahm array of 0 for example times 2. Ok, that's going to print out my first number multiplied by 2 and that's what we want and I could just do this five different times for each of the elements here. But first of all that's a very impractical and inefficient way of doing things. And second of all, what if my array was like a hundred or thousand elements long? Well then that's a thousand extra lines of code we have to write which would take ages to write and is just horribly ugly and inefficient. Luckily for us we can actually write this exact line of code, put it in a loop and let the loop do all the work for us. Now if we're clever we can actually do the same thing. We can do this with a while loop. We will just have to create an extra indexing variable but it's much easier with a for loop. So I'll show you how to do that. We start off with a 4. And now we'll follow it with something interesting since X so just bear with me here and I'll explain what's going on. Once I finish writing this. So in actuality let's say this for Nahm in the Nahm array. We are simply going to print out and actually I'm just going to take this and just paste it right in here. But I'm going to change some array of 0 to array of times to oh and this should be numb. There we go. So now it's complete. Now this is kind of weird syntax. If you are not used to it, allow me to explain what is going on. So we're basically saying for something in Namah right and now there's a saying for each of the elements within marae when it comes to that element we're going to call it numb. So at the beginning and then we're going to execute this on each of those at the beginning. Nahm is going to jump to the first element in this array. Because this is a for loop and that's how they work. They start at the beginning and finish at the end. So numb would take on the value of 13 because this is saying 13 is the first element. OK we are at the beginning of the loop and the array. So Nahm is going to equal 30. And now we're just going to print. And not sure why we went when indexes should actually just be Nahm times too. Apologies for the faulty syntax there. So this is just going to take a value Nahm currently holds times up by 2 and then prints it out. Now once we finish up we'll get to the second value in number 8 which is 53 again. Now will equal 53 will Prince 53 times to then a third value Nahm is to print that term to then number 67 then number 9 and then after that we say AK Nahm array is finished. There are no more elements in it. So then we go on to X out of this loop. So this is why it works so well with arrays and lists is because we can simply say for each of the elements within this array or list we're going to call this variable and have it take on the value that we're currently on in the array and then we're just going to do something with it in the loop. So if I were to execute this I get these numbers being printed out. I start with 26 and 1 to 6. Then for the 134 then 18 so it's essentially exactly doubled. Each of these numbers. Now the great thing about four loops versus something like a while loop is I know exactly how many times it's going to run. Also I know it's going to start at the beginning of my array. It's going to end at the end of my array and it's going to visit every single element within my array. Now that's not the same for while loops we have to design the code very carefully when doing essentially the same thing in a while loop.

And that's because we might not necessarily know where to start in the loop. We might not know where the loop ends and maybe again we'd have to create some kind of an indexing variable. This on the other hand is kind of doing all of that for us. It's saying OK so numb is equal to Naama array of 0. We're going to do that then numb is equal to the number of one that will do that. Then two and three then four. And that's that, I guess or any five elements. All right. So those are the basics of flips, just a really handy way to visit each of the elements within an array and then do something based on that. Now it's similar to our IF statements where we had nested if statements here. We can actually have nested loops. So if I had like an array of arrays and I wanted to iterate through that I probably use nested loops to do so but nested loops can get a Lessel complex and can be very slow. So as much as possible, choose to avoid doing that. However in some situations it is just the only way we can solve the problem. Otherwise that is your basic loop intro.

```python
trafficLightState = "yellow"
distanceFromLight = 10

# if trafficLightState == "green":
#     print("go")
# elif trafficLightState == "yellow" and distanceFromLight <= 15:
#     print("speed up")
# elif trafficLightState == "yellow" and distanceFromLight > 15:
#     print("slow down")
# elif trafficLightState == "red":
#     print("stop")
# else:
#     print("unknown action")

if trafficLightState == "green":
    print("go")
elif trafficLightState == "yellow":
    if distanceFromLight <= 15:
        print("speed up")
    else:
        print("slow down")
elif trafficLightState == "red":
    print("stop")
else:
    print("unknown action")

endPoint = 10
startPoint = 3
currentPos = startPoint
print(currentPos)

while currentPos < endPoint:
    currentPos += 1
    print(currentPos)

numArray = [13,53,2,67,9]

for num in numArray:
    print(num * 2)
```

```
Control Flow
/Library/Frameworks/Python.framework/Versions/3.6/bin/python3.6 "/Users/owl/Deskt
speed up
3
4
5
6
7
8
9
10
26
106
4
134
18

Process finished with exit code 0
```

So as always to be sure it's a lot of practice. I know loops can be a. I know they can be a weird and difficult concept to understand especially if you've never seen loops before. So you definitely want to practice a lot with them. But essentially we use while loops when we don't necessarily know how many times we're going to run. And we use for in loops or for loops when we want to straight through array elements all we want to specify a range and know exactly how many times you want to run. So for example I could do something like range 0 4 and just do something like that instead. Before in loops, loops are best used when we know exactly how many times they are going to run. So with the conclusion of loops comes the conclusion. Also our control slows S.. So we covered just the IF. ELSE. Statements in their slight variations and then be covered while loops and finished up with four loops so be sure to write some practice of your own. Again Python's really good for just right and quick code and running it and kind of demonstrating how the concepts work. So once you are comfortable using the if else of an L statements and then while and for loops Let's move on to the next section which will be dealing with basic functions and be sure to try and test stuff like nested for loops and while loops and then stuff like a nested if statement and then and in all operations as well.

EXAMPLE CODE

Control flow statements dictate how your Python code executes. Here are some examples:

1. if statement:

Python
age = 18

```
if age >= 18:
  print("You are eligible to vote.")
else:
  print("You are not eligible to vote.")
```
Use code with caution.
This code checks if age is greater than or equal to 18. If true, it prints "You are eligible to vote", otherwise it prints "You are not eligible to vote."

2. if-elif-else statement:

Python
```
grade = 85

if grade >= 90:
  print("Excellent!")
elif grade >= 80:
  print("Great job!")
else:
  print("Keep practicing!")
```
Use code with caution.
This code uses an if-elif-else chain to evaluate grades. It prints "Excellent!" for grades 90 or above, "Great job!" for grades 80 or above (but less than 90), and "Keep practicing!" for anything lower.

3. for loop:

Python
```
fruits = ["apple", "banana", "cherry"]

for fruit in fruits:
  print(f"I like {fruit}.")
```
Use code with caution.
This code iterates through the fruits list using a for loop. For each item in the list (fruit), it prints a message with the fruit name.

4. while loop:

Python
```
count = 0

while count < 5:
  print(f"Count: {count}")
  count += 1  # Increment count by 1

print("Loop finished.")
```
Use code with caution.
This code uses a while loop that continues as long as count is less than 5. It prints the current value of count and then increments it before checking the loop condition again.

5. break and continue statements:

These statements are used to control loop flow:

break: Exits the loop completely.
continue: Skips the current iteration and moves to the next.
Here's an example using break:

Python
```
for number in range(10):
  if number == 7:
    print(f"Found number: {number}")
    break  # Exit the loop when number is 7
  else:
    print(f"Checking: {number}")
```
Use code with caution.
This code iterates from 0 to 9, but the loop exits with a break when it finds the number 7.

Remember, these are just basic examples. Control flow statements can be combined to create complex program logic!

FUNCTIONS

Pay guys previously we explore the concepts of control flow which essentially provided us a way to choose which blocks of code we want to execute based on the outcome offsets and tests. We saw that even with loops although they might not look like they're performing the test necessarily every time they have to perform some tests at the beginning of each Llopis ration to determine whether or not to continue on or to exit out of the loop. Well now we're going to explore an even more convenient mechanism to choose which blocks of code we want to execute. And we won't have to perform any tests to do so. This is all going to be done through the use of functions. Now there's a couple of great things about functions. The first is that we can't just define the function once and continue to call upon that function over and over again. So that way if our function is complex and contains many lines of code we don't have to write those lines of code to perform the same function every single time we can just call upon the function name Palsson any promises if necessary and that the function that has already been defined. Do all the work for us. The second great thing about functions is that they provide a nice sense of organization to our code so we can kind of group together. Nice. Replacing it blocks off statements so that it's easy to find the pieces of code that we want because we know for example a function is going to perform this task. So if whatever reason task A is messing up we know it's probably something to do with function. And finally we get very fine Choon over exactly when and where we want to execute the code rather than having to rely on the outcome of tests or just kind of printing the code willy nilly. So the topic of functions is actually a fairly straightforward one. Probably easier than control flow. And we're only going to really explore a few concepts in this topic. So the first is just going to explore some basic functions syntax in Python and we'll take a look at how to not only create functions and fill them with code but also how to call upon them and run the code inside execute that code that will take a look at parameters and finally finish up with return values. Now provinces are just values that we pass into a function and return values of values or a value that a function might output. Once it finishes running. So I think we get started with an interesting example and this is basically going to take in an array of numbers. This function will add it's going to multiply all those numbers together and then it's going to output the result. Now I want to do a sum function which is going to add all the numbers together. The functionality exists; we can actually just call some and then put in a bunch of numbers. But like I said we want to keep things different. So I'm going to have a multiplier function. So because Python is pretty easy to run we can actually do all of this stuff without the use of a function. But once we put inside of a function we'll see that this is going to be a much better way of doing things. And that's going to be to use functions as much as possible. So we'll start with just some variables here. The first is just going to be our array and it is going to set this equal to an array of numbers so we'll just have the first five numbers here. Okay. And then we can have a variable called total or something. I'll just say that this is 0 for now. So hopefully from our discussion on control flow and on arrays you guys have a general sense of how you might go about doing this centrally. We will use a loop and we'll just take each of these elements and multiply it by the total which I guess should actually start out as one. And at the end we can just print that out. And in fact print is itself a function that we've been using all along. But more on that in Elisabet I just want to sum up how a basic loop works. Let's just go for an array. We are simply going to say total multiply equals numbness. And then at the very end we can just print out the value of total. Let's go and zoom out and before we run this again I'm working in another file. This is called the function dot pi. I have it set up from my control flow. As you can see. So let's just run functions instead. If you want to choose the same file that's fine again just comment how all of the old code is running functions. I get the value of 120 printed out which is correct because one times two times three times more times five should be equal to 120. Now the annoying thing is that every single time I once worked SECU this code. I then have to call on this and I have to basically copy and paste code over and over again. Now this isn't a ton of code right here. But imagine if our function had let's say like a dozen lines of code and every time we wanted to execute that code we would have to write out that same dozen lines. Well wouldn't it be much easier if we just stuck the sole on one function so that every time you want to execute the code we simply call upon the function like we would our print statement here and execute that code within. So the way we would go about doing this is to start with death. And this is how we start our functions. Now functions need a name. This one is going to cool because something like multiply. OK following the name com brackets. And usually we put our parameters inside of these brackets. But in this case we're not going to have any to start off with so we can add them in later. Now similar to control flow at the end we want to add our code to signify the end of the function name and parameters and then we want to put the function body within the function itself. So what I'm going to do is actually take all this stuff here. And actually you know what, let's take the whole loss of it. I'm just going to cast it and just paste it right within our multiply function and can squish this all together and that should be good for now. Now I'm not including numb array in my function because this is something that might change later on if I put an array within my function then it's going to be performing the same operation on the exact same array every single time. This way I can push for multiplication on arrays later on. I can then change the name array to be some completely different array such as you know five six seven and eight. And then I can call multiply on that function again. Or rather could multiply on that array. So now let's see what happens if we run this code. Well nothing's printed out but nothing was printed out. We've clearly said print total here and we know that this has been working before. Well the problem here is that we haven't called upon the function. We've only declared it or defined it. So if we want to actually call upon multiply and execute all of this code we have to make a call to it simply by saying multiply. So if we go to run this now we get 120 printed out because this call to multiply is going to go to most place definitions. It's going to find any it's going to pass in any parameters in this case there are none. And then is going to execute all of the code found within. So it's going to total everything. And then just print that out. Similarly if I then called multiply on this array then I should get yet another value being printed out. So I ran this. And then as you can see two different values because now the array has this value up top and then changes its value later around. So you can see the benefit of using these functions. I can just play almost every single time rather than how to write the code for each case where a rate changes its value. Now this function isn't very flexible because we are not making any promises. And also we're only taking in Numb arrays so it's if we defined a different kind of array such as let's say something slightly different name number array and I set the sequel to you know like 10 11 12 13 and then I could multiply again and multiply is not going to do anything with number array because I've said that our most play function is only ever going to work on this numb array here which is going to be this variable is where promises can come in really handy if we added a parameter to this function then we eliminate the need for this extra variable altogether and we can choose to execute this function on any array we want as long as we pass it into the function when we call upon it. So I'm going to go ahead and completely redefine it while not completely redefining our function. I'm just going to modify it a bit and have it take a variable called Nahm array. This way I can actually eliminate this and I can just get rid of all of this stuff here. So now this should give me an error or some kind of annoyance saying well we kind of expected to take in some kind of a parameter here. So why are we not taking anything in? So now if you'll see if I start to cool multiply now I need to enter in some kind of number array here. So in this case I'm just going to answer in some random array. Let's just stick with what we had before. Just the numbers 1 through 5. So if we go to run it we should get the same results before 120. Similarly if I ran it with some different numbers I think we had 5 6 7 8 was the next one. And we had like 600 or something that I got to run it. Yep 16 AC again. So we know that this is working exactly as it should. So the benefit of adding this promise at the end is that we don't have to declare those extra variables anymore. And now every time I call upon multiply all I need to do is pass in the exact values I want to multiply together and then I'm good to go. So this is a much better way of defining this function than what we had going on previously. So the thing we put in here is called a parameter. This is essentially something that we have to pass into the function every time we call upon it. And it's also something that we're using clearly in the code itself. So what this means is when we call upon multiplication and the Palsson numb array takes on this value that we pulsated. So now we're saying for Nahm in this array it's 5 6 7 8 will execute this code here. Similarly bypassed in some completely different values like 50 4 6 3 and 10 then number array takes on these values here and I'm not going to run on this because I'll produce quite a large number and we've already seen how it works. Anyway now this functions pretty well but we can actually go one step further and make it even better even more flexible. So right now it is totaling everything just fine and is printing the total. But that's it. It's not like we can actually do anything with that total. So instead what we can have this function do is return something it can return the total so that we can do whatever we want without Tosha later on. We can add something to it. We can subtract something from it. We can multiply it to something else we can print out. So on and so forth. So all we really need to do here is get rid of this print code and we'll just go and say return total. So now all functions once it finishes executing we'll do this, do our loop elects with the loop and it will get to this and it will basically say OK we're going to return this fall. We're going to spit some value out once we finish executing. So now I'm going to call him my function but I can also store the results because it's returning a value in some kind of a variable. So he can say something like results equals multiplying with these numbers. I'm going to go back to the simple version 1 through 5 and then at the end I can print the results if I want. So as you can see I got to run this and now I get once when 20 being printed out even though I'm not actually printing anything in the function it sells. That's because dysfunctions executing on this array to the top being the parameter and then is going to return the total value and stort end result which would then be princeling if we wanted to do the shorthand we could actually just print a call to multiply here. So it could just take this copy and paste it in and eliminate the need for my result variable and will do exactly the same thing. So now that we've covered return values and promises and the basics of functions that is pretty much all we have to discuss on this topic. Like you said it's a bit easier to understand than some folk control flow stuff particularly the loops. It's essentially just a convenient way to store our code just to quickly summarize if we want to define our function. We start with desks. We give the function a name. The brackets here with any promises that code on to signify that the function body is beginning and then we put the function body in here. Basically the code we want to execute when the function is called we call upon the function by simply typing its name in the brackets beside the function. We just put the values that we once Palsson as the parameter then prompts all values that we pass in that can be used throughout the function body itself just like any other variable. But they only take on value when we pass the value in as a parameter. We also have functions where return values will basically output something once they reach this return statement. And by the way this return statement doesn't have to be at the end of the function. We just need to make sure that if the function is going to return something it will always return something in all possible cases. We didn't in these examples. Well actually we did with the flu but we can make these functions as complex as we want by. And again lots of control flow. So we can add in loops as we did here. We can add in stuff like if statements. We can even make calls to other functions within the function body itself. Just know that if you want to return something from a function when you call upon it a result will be outputted which we can then use in this case with simply printing out. But we could use that value as we would any other variable.

```python
# Functions
# Parameters
# Return values


def multiply(numArray):
    total = 1
    for num in numArray:
        total *= num
    return total

print(multiply([1,2,3,4,5]))
```

Otherwise that wraps up functions nicely and we can move on to our next topic which is going to be classes. So play around with functions Elisabet try to simulate some scenarios in which you think you might need functions. A good place to start would be some kind of a simple video game to implement stuff like play movements. What to do if the player collides with something or just some simple game mechanics that's always a fun and practical example to go on. So once you get familiar with functions let's move on to Klaus's.

EXAMPLE CODE

1. Simple Function:

Python
```
def greet(name):
  """Greets the user by name."""
  message = f"Hello, {name}!"
  print(message)

greet("Alice")  # Call the function with an argument
```
Use code with caution.
This code defines a function named greet that takes one argument (name). It creates a message using an f-string and prints it. The function is then called with the argument "Alice".

2. Function with Multiple Arguments and Return Value:

Python
```
def calculate_area(length, width):
  """Calculates the area of a rectangle."""
  area = length * width
  return area

rectangle_area = calculate_area(5, 3)  # Call the
```

function and store the return value
print(f"Area of the rectangle: {rectangle_area}")
Use code with caution.
This code defines a function calculate_area that takes two arguments (length and width). It calculates the area and returns the result using the return statement. The function is called with arguments 5 and 3, and the returned area is stored in the rectangle_area variable before being printed.

3. Default Arguments:

Python
```
def greet(name="World"):
  """Greets the user by name (default: World)."""
  message = f"Hello, {name}!"
  print(message)

greet()  # Call without argument uses default value
greet("Bob")  # Call with argument
```
Use code with caution.
This code defines a function greet with a default argument for name. If no argument is provided when calling the function, the default value "World" is used.

These are just a few examples of functions in Python. They are a powerful tool for modularizing your code and making it more reusable and readable.

CLASSES AND WRAP UP

What's up guys having just finished our discussion on functions I think we now know enough to start taking a look at our final topic which is going to be on classes and objects. So this is not just going to be our last topic but it's also going to bring together everything that we've learned in the previous four sections. So if there's anything from those sections you're unsure about, definitely go. That being said, this is going to be a nice way to bring everything together. So some of it will be reviewed and some of that will be covering entirely new concepts. So we'll just divide our discussion on classes and objects into our will for five main parts so we get started first by talking about what a class is, what an object is and what the relationship is between the two. Then we'll take a look at how to add properties to our class. We'll do this with variables. Then take a look at how to add behaviors to the class. This will be done through the use of functions and methods. Then we'll start exploring the concepts of using initializers which are a special type of function that help us create new instances of classes. I'll explain what these mean. A little later on. And finally we'll finish up our scutcheon on this topic with the concepts of inheritance which essentially provides a way from one class to inherit all of another class's attributes. Now as always I've started a new style. This one is called class system pi. So if you start a new file then I encourage you to do so. Otherwise just comment out all the old stuff. And for me I'm just going to make sure that when I run my new file I am indeed running classes rather than any of the previous ones so running this will just produce a blank rerun screen. So let's get started by talking about what classes and objects are and what the relationship is between the two. Now so far all of the values we've seen have kind of been just single values or multiple values in the case of stuff like arrays and tuples. But that's really all that holding is a specific value rather than representing an entire object. So for example if we use a string that represents let's say a pencil or someone's name that string isn't representing the object itself it's just the name that we've given to the person or the name of the object. Similarly if we store a number within a variable that's not representing an object that's just some value that that variable currently holds. And the same could be applied to tuples and lists; these are just kinds of lists of values or tuples of values; these aren't necessarily objects themselves. Well this is where things are going to get a little different because we can use objects to represent entire real world objects such as a bicycle or an animal or in the example we're going to be using an entire video game character. Now objects typically represent weird States and behavior and so states can be interchange with prophecies here. So state and proxies are represented with variables and these will hold individual values that will help to build our objects up. And then the behaviors of the objects are represented through the use of functions or is there asserts who once were in classes as methods. So from now onwards I want us to start thinking about a video game character and what kind of properties or attributes this character might have and what behaviors he or she might be able to carry out. For example some straightforward and simple properties a character might have or something like a name maybe character has a number of hit points maybe a character has a certain position on the map a certain strength or something and so on and so forth where some behaviors might be two moves forwards or backwards to change on the current hit points and so on and so forth so try to think about some properties and behaviors a character might have. Now as for what a class is, the class is just a code representation of the object so we can kind of think about the class as being the blueprints that represent the objects and then the object being the value of that particular class, specifically an object is considered in an instance of a class. So whereas a class might define all of the behavior that an object should have as well as all of the properties that an object should have. The object is how we actually store specific values in those particular properties. So to help demonstrate this point when we launch right into an example we'll start by just creating a basic video game character class and then we can start to add more properties and more behaviors as we go. So the way we start with class declarations is by typing class we give the class a name and this naming convention is a little different from usual. And in this case we're actually going to capsulize names so we'll call this something like a game character. And by the way I just want to keep this fairly generic right now because we don't get a little more specific later on so these should be attributes that would be common across all game characters. So whether those game characters or non-player characters or play characters or just something simple. So with the name we put the code on and then we put the actual class definition underneath just like we would any other function or control flow and so on and so forth. So some process of game Carrot's might have would be something like a name OK which is just going to be a blank string now or Additionally we can actually say none. It doesn't really matter but I'll just say a blank string just because we want to communicate that this should be a string and not a number. So a video game character might also have something like a maximum number of hit points or max hit points. Just going to set the sequence to zero for now. Similarly they'll have a current hit points value. And this is also going to be 0 for now. And then the character might also have something like an x position. So I'm not going to bother with X and Y positions. Let's just assume that this is just kind of moving left and right now just going to really keep things simple. Hence why I'm going to stick with these four attributes. Now I know a game character could have dozens and dozens of different attributes and effects of a built in natural game. Obviously I'd add a little more than this but we're just trying to keep things simple and straightforward as possible. So as of right now we've created a class and we've given some properties to this class. Now these are represented with our basic variables as we've seen before. Alternatively we can actually have lists as our values so if I had like an inventory of items that might be a list of items and also we can have other classes of objects as global variables or as properties of the class but we might save that for the end now not how none of these hold any real values right now. I mean not to say that zeros aren't necessarily real values but they don't really represent anything in the context of current and maximum hit points that might get an x position. But we definitely shouldn't have max hit points of 0. Similarly this is just a blank string for the name right now.

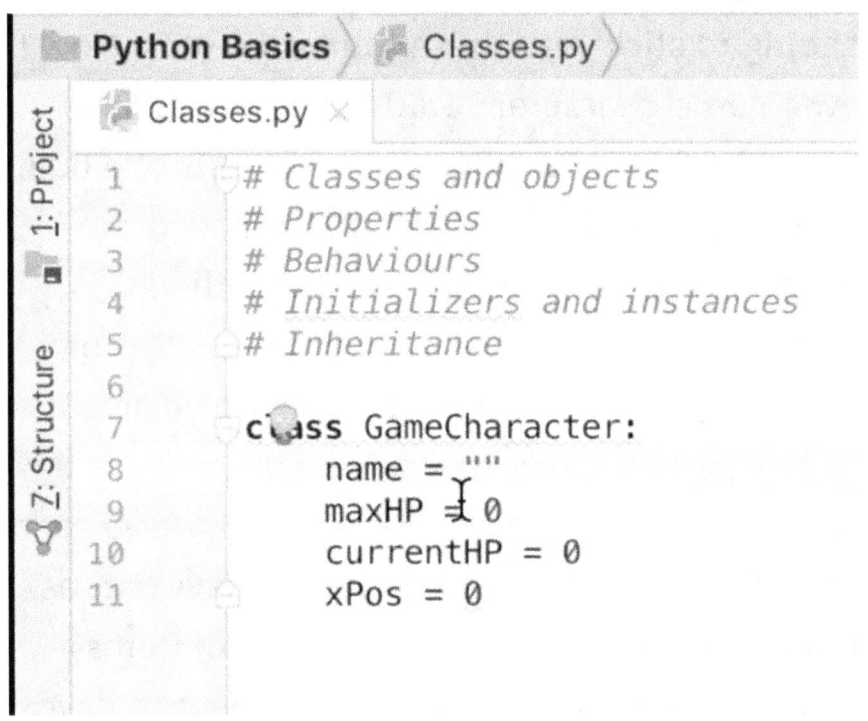

Well we'll actually use what's called an initializer to give some values. But I'm going to come back to the initializer a little later on. Let's first just get this class up and running with some behaviors. Then we'll come back to the concepts of initializations and instances. So what behaviors might our videogame characters have? Well most of the functions and the methods that we add inside of the class are used to modify the character state or modify the properties. So these are often called states instead of proxies because they helped to represent the current values that a particular object can hold. We're going to see there's a little Bessa once we start talking about the objects themselves and instances just know that when I use what states of prophecy I'm kind of talking about these global variables up here. So let's just create a couple of pretty simple functions. One is going to change our current hit points and one is going to change our x position so we can create a function starting with definition. And this one is just going to be called something like change. Hit points. And we are going to take in some parameters. Note the use of the word self so I'll get back to this in just a second here. And I'm just going to add an additional pram. Just make sure that you don't delete this. We do need self as should add ALL SO BASICALLY anyway. So rather than making this function a set of current hit points I'm actually going to add or put in a value that will increase or decrease our current hit points. So I'm just going to say something like change in his points and in our function definition or in the implementation itself we're just going to put something like cells dots. We have to do Cells dolt's card points if we want access to this. And again I'll explain why in just a second and we're just going to say plus equals change in hit points. So essentially this function, if it's called on an instance of a game character, is just going to take on some value. Let's say for example 50 or Hundred and it's just going to add that value to the current hit points value of the hit points of 50. We had 50 pulse and 50 instance functions and our current hit points would then be 100. Assuming that everything works out well here now. Note the key use of this word self. So self refers to the class that we currently work in again.

For example, we work on game characters right now. Everything here belongs to a game character class. This means when I call self don't current hit points I'm referring to this card current hit points up here. The current hit points up belong to this particular class. Now if I actually just tried to type in current hit points there's not even an option that I can work with. I have sickle cell Dalt. If I want access to any of the functions or the prophecies of this class Similarly any of the functions that belong to a particular class begin with self as the first parameter. Now that's just something that is added automatically and is a property of any of the classes that again belong to a specific function of the functions that belong to a specific class. Whereas we saw before, if we were to have some kind of function here, a random sunk cave, then it would not require the use of the word cells. And actually in a lot of languages the self keyword is unnecessary in some cases but in Python We actually have to use that word. OK so with this in mind we'll design our other function which is going to do very similar things for our exposition. So it can change position or change. Pause that works. Kate will open up the brackets again, cells added automatically. And I was just going to say change and ex-POWs. I guess I should be specific. This is changing our exposition. And we're just going to say self-taught Currence who actually is sulpha exposition plus equals change in position. All right. So for a lot of these variables you'll often see something like this. You'll see the global variable itself and then you'll see functions that do something like this, for example get x position. And this is just going to do something like return self-taught exposition to ex-POWs. Similarly you might see something like this. Def sets position. OK and again this is probably going to take in some new value. So X pause and then we could just say self-taught X pause equals new ex-POWs. So this is one good way of doing things but it's not necessary to do this 100 percent of the time. For the most part the reason we would create these separate guesser accesses as they cooled is because they're just guessing of value and assessing a value is if we're making these variables private now private variables are essentially only accessible within the class itself.

So if I declared some of these variables as private and then tried to access them outside of my class definition then I couldn't do so. They don't even appear as options. For the most part making variables private in Python is actually discouraged. Whereas in some other languages it is encouraged. I know in Java as much as possible we should try to restrict access to variables but in something like Python which is kind of weird it's encouraged to make everything accessible. As much as possible and avoid the use of private variables if we really want to make variables private we actually precede the variable name itself with these two onda schools here. And if we want to indicate that these variables are accessible we can change our values. But we should probably use separate functions to do so. We can actually just add the single underscore. And this is not technically restricting the access but it's kind of saying that. Be careful if you are trying to access this variable. If you want to use this then probably create the separate gasa ancestor functions. So because I'm actually ok with these being accessible everywhere and I'm not going to. I don't really want to create separate Geza and SESA functions for all four of these variables. I'm actually just going to get rid of this and make these variables available everywhere. That way we can access them directly by calling on an instance named dot name or dot max hit points or so on and so forth and just get and change the value that way. OK so when we're changing our hit points we should probably place some restrictions on the maximum and minimum hit points minimum of values that hit point can take on as well we should probably restrict the expositions to maintain within the boundaries of some kind of a map but I don't know how big or small the map is. So I'm only going to focus on my change hit points now. So in this function we might want to say something like. And we can say something like self Dot's current hit points is greater than our self taught max hit points. Well in this case we just want to set self-taught current hit points equal to self-styled max hit points so this is essentially saying that we can never go over our maximum number of hit points and then similarly we can say something along the lines of I s self-taught current hit points is less than zero. OK well in this case we're just going to say Celso current hit points equals zero and the additional behaviors such as deleting lives, removing the characters from the game and so on and so forth. But I'm not going to implement it here again for two reasons, one because I'm trying to keep things simple and because I'm actually going to add in some of that behavior a little later on where it will be a little more appropriate. For now I just want to kind of restrict the values to remain within a certain range. OK so we've essentially added some properties and some behaviors to this class so we can now change our characters' hit points.

```python
class GameCharacter:
    name = ""
    maxHP = 0
    currentHP = 0
    xPos = 0

    def changeHP(self, changeInHP):
        self.currentHP += changeInHP
        if self.currentHP > self.maxHP:
            self.currentHP = self.maxHP
        elif self.currentHP < 0:
            self.currentHP = 0

    def changeXPos(self, changeInXPos):
        self.xPos += changeInXPos
```

We can change a kerchief's exposition and it's as if the Skerritt is healing up or being injured and then moving about the map as well at any point in time. Our character will have these attributes with some actual values in them. So how do we set up a new instance of a game character so essentially create a new game character object because this is just the class definition right now. Well to do so we need what's called an initializer which is a very special type of function. This will help us to create what are called new instances of game characters and then populate some of the necessary values. So right off the bat our game character typically will have some of the values set up as soon as he or she is created. So there should be stuff like a name, maximum current hit points and a certain position on the map. That's why I added only these four. Additionally we might have something like an inventory of items which should probably be initialized to be empty as a character when first born probably won't have anything in the inventory. Similarly it'd be maybe like a skill set or a certain amount of damage or so on and so forth.

The strength of character might have. These are going to be initial values to a Karatz it needs to have as soon as it's created. And we're going to use our initialiser to help set them up. So if we actually start typing in dash in it he'll notice that we get a few different functions being pulled up so we actually want this one here which is just going to be our very basic initialiser Now note right now that it's not taking in any promises other than self because of course self always has to be the what we want is to actually pulse in some families for these variables because we want to set the values as soon as the Initialize is called. So we're just going to take in some parameters like we would any other variable and name will take a maximum hit points and will take in a current exposition. So to set these values will simply say something like a self-taught name equals the name that is repulsing into the here. Will say self dots. A note actually. This is an ASP. OK so this. These belong to the class itself. So if I type in max hit points then I still know that I belong to this class and then I say equal to max at points here. No that it's a pity because this is a parameter now. So that's how we know I'm talking about this Max hit points especially because it's self-taught max hit points this one. And then the max hit points obsessing equal to is just this one here. OK self-taught exposition is now going to be our expedition we pass in and we just need our current hit points next so we're actually going to say Celta current hit points is just equal to our Max at points. Whoops. Max hit points as well which makes sense we want to start our cars 100 percent healthy. All right. So that's a basic initialiser. Every time we create a new instance of a game character we call on this initialiser. I'll show you how to do that in a second. Then we Palsson these initial values and it just sets a character up as he or she was first born and just has those kinds of base values. So with this initialiser to find we can now go ahead and create some new instances of our class. Let's just get rid of that. We'll be outside of our class declaration right now as well making sure that we are not indented all using space as a tool and will store this new instance in something that's very similar to a variable. So I'm just going to call this something like a new game character. And I'm going to set this equal to. I saw its opening game character. This clause comes up. So I typed in and it's as if I'm using an initializer function. I'm just going to open up the parameters like it would and it's going to ask for a name maximum hit points and an x position. So I'm just going to start by typing in my own name. I'll give this guy let's say 100 hit points to start off with and we'll start this play. It's this character position one. So then we've successfully created an instance of a game character class which is an object. And this is our new game character objects so you'll note that it looks very similar to a typical variable declaration. It's kind of as if we are pulsing in the value of a game character and it just has each of these values stored within it. So the value of this class right now is kind of the sum of all of these properties. So this is essentially called on our initialiser to know how we're passing and name a maximum number of points on an exposition. So as of right now our game character has the value here as Nimish now has the maximum hit points as 100. Same with the current hit points and then the x position is 1. So if I were to print these values out so prints plus or so if I were to print my new game character I don't really get anything printed out but I could create a separate print function to do so. But let's just print out the attributes one by one so it came with a character dot name. We can print new game characters towards the current hit points or maximum hit points doesn't matter. This is to the current hit points and that we can print the new character towards x position so zooming out going to go hadn't run this. And as you can see I get my appropriate values being printed here. So this is how we access the values within a class and we access the functions in exactly the same way. So for example if I wanted to change my hit points they tried to change it. Let's say we'll subtract 50 from our hit points. Might we sustain some damage. So I'm going to say new game character thoughts change. Hit points. OK I'm going to add in a change and hit points in this case next of 50 and I'm going to print out my characters hit points again to see if things have changed. So current hit points so we'll give this a run. And as you can see my current hit points are now 50. And if I try to set that over a hundred or less than zero the restrictions would be put in place and make sure that doesn't happen. OK so if you have some functions to modify the values we can actually modify the values directly by saying something like new game character dots X exposition equals let's say 50. For some reason and then I want to print out when you character to x position. OK well go ahead and run that and see the Exposition is now 50 as well. And this is certainly one way of doing things. The reason we actually have direct access to these variables and can change values is again because I'm not making them private. I'm not really restricting the access at all. So the only reason we would want to restrict the access this way is if we don't want to be able to do this we don't want to accidentally change the values on that particular object and just want to be careful to use the separate functions such as Geza and Sessa functions to help us to do so. So at the end of the day it really just comes down to personal preference how you want to do things. But like I said Python does kind of encourage you to make things as open and as accessible as possible which is kind of different from some of the other languages. Now so far we've covered basically four or five main concepts so the only one that we have left to explore is going to be the concepts of inheritance so inheritance is basically one class inheriting all of the other classes' properties and functions methods as well as the initializations. Now this is important because it will save us having to essentially implement the same class twice as well. The subclause which is what inherits from the superclass can define additional properties and additional functions of the road. So the reason I made my game character fairly generic and just how stuff like change hit points change x position haven't made any special behaviors here except to restrict this within a range. That's a very simple property because I now want to create a new class called play a character. So typically in a game we might have player and non-player characters the player character will generally have a lot more proxies and a lot more functionality than a non player character because obviously we're going to be interacting and controlling that character. So we want a player to be able to have everything that a game character can have but it wants to have more as well that might be more behavior's more props. Adam I actually want to change the way these functions work a little bit. So let's start by creating our subclass of game characters. Again I'm going to call this play character will define some properties of its own and will even override a couple of the methods which is essentially going to be providing a slightly different implementation for some of these functions. So I'm going to define it right below. Arwa originally classed the game character and we define subclasses in a very very similar way. I'm going to give this a name. Play a character now it needs a note as a subclause by putting in the brackets the name of the superclass in this case. Game character. OK so now if you'll notice I'm just going to add one proxy to that goes away. And this is just going to be a number of lives of those lives. Whoops. Not live as we want. And we're going to set the sequel to zero. OK so now because this is inherited from game characters, not only the properties up here but also this initialiser and these functions. I can actually create an instance of my play character.

```
    def changeHP(self,changeInHP):
        self.currentHP += changeInHP
        if self.currentHP > self.maxHP:
            self.currentHP = self.maxHP
        elif self.currentHP < 0:
            self.currentHP = 0

    def changeXPos(self,changeInXPos):
        self.xPos += changeInXPos

class PlayerCharacter(GameCharacter):
    lives = 0

newGameCharacter = GameCharacter("Nimish",100,1)
print(newGameCharacter.name)
print(newGameCharacter.currentHP)
print(newGameCharacter.xPos)
newGameCharacter.changeHP(-50)
print(newGameCharacter.currentHP)
newGameCharacter.xPos = 50
print(newGameCharacter.xPos)
```

So just going to get started actually by deleting all of these because I don't want them to create my new play a character play a character this time this is going to be a play a character instance we can open up the brackets here. And again we can use the same constructs as before we put in the name Max hit points and exposition. So if I put in some name let's go with something like KC on a first name that came to mind. This one has 150 hit points this time and starts exposition 10. Now again I have access to all of the same properties. This time I need to call a new play a character talk for example my current hit points. If I want to print this out, I could do so as just run this 150 being printed out because I'm now putting printing on you play characters hit points but it would be kind of pointless to do this if I didn't go and find new stuff within this class. And this is kind of the whole purpose of this subclause super close relationship and inheritance is the ability to get everything a particular class has and then implement more stuff. Again the whole idea behind this relationship is to eliminate the need to implement exactly the same stuff multiple times because that's actually pretty bad code practice if you're doing the same stuff you're right and exactly the same code over and over again. There's probably a more efficient way to do that. If that's the case. So let's just go about and redefine some of these attributes here. So for example our new play a character might have lives and also might have let's say an inventory inventory here and I'm just going to set this equal to an empty you know what let's make a dictionary because it makes a little more sense. Actually you know what in the interest of keeping things simple I'm just going to actually make this an array with a bunch of Dyson's in it. So now I play a character that has these additional two attributes which I can access. So for example you play a character dots lives. OK I can access that. But what I can't do is say you game character dot lives because that doesn't exist on our new game character that's only a proxy of play a character. So whereas the subclause gains everything that superclass has not necessarily the other way around. So my goal here is to set these two values up. So in order to do so I'm going to need to provide a new definition for my initialiser because I want to initialize my inventory with maybe a couple of different items such as a shirt and pants or something. And then we also want to set this Carrot's up with a few lights or Z having zero lives is bad. So the way we would do this is by defining yet another initialiser so deaths and that's We start with self again. We want to take in the same three values as before but we want to take in some additional values or at the very least set these values up. So actually we weren't taking some additional inventory values or additional number of lives we're going to say each of these play characters with a default three lives and a default in inventory with two items in it. So we'll take in the name we'll take in a max hit points we'll take in a current x position and now we're going to need to first call upon the superclasses initialiser and then set up our additional stuff. Now the reason we're calling on the super close initialiser is again to avoid writing the same code twice now. Cool on this and it's actually giving me this error saying it needs to cool hours superclass the way I get around this is by calling my supa OK and how oh wow I actually filled in all fours automatically. So we need the super keyword in the brackets. We need that class that we're working in to play a character. We need the sell key. And then we call it DOT. And then we Palsson the same values like we were like we would if we we're calling on the initialiser here. So in this case the values will be passed again will be our name max hit points on our exposition. So now essentially what this will accomplish is when we call on our initialiser we're still pulser to name hit points and x position and now it's essentially going to invoke the superclasses called this and it will perform the same initializing as before. But now we can define additional stuff such as self. Self-taught lives. Siri can actually spell that equals three. And then they can say something like Salto inventory equals just some array with some items and is going to say something like shirts and pants. Now I want to see if this would be best represented with the dictionary because then we could have quantities of these items but let's just keep things simple. If I were to just use my default superclasses initialiser I'm actually just going to comment this out quickly and then I would print my new play characters and lives. And Amaterasu mountain runs this. Now it gets 0 here. That's because I'm not using this initialiser yet. And I just set my life up to be zero. But now let's say that I do want to use my actual initialiser here. So what's going on in this. So lives should have the value of three because we're using our soup our subclauses initialiser here which is cool and super close initialiser but also setting this stuff up. Then if I now run this I get the value of three. The number of lives because we use this initialiser. And at the same time I still get 150 because I'm using my superclasses initialiser as well in this cool here's super taught in its And that's how we call anything in the superclass is just going to be the super dark in it and that will just cool super dot whatever is super don't change hit points or change x position or name and so on and so forth. And that's how we access the superclasses version of that. So in let's build a power play a character gets closer a little bit more. We'll define a separate function that will just add an inventory item. So this could be something like adding inventory Isom and we can take in a new item that should have the space there and it should really be adding spaces here it just makes the code a bit more readable. Just kind of trying to save some time. So in this case we are just going to take ourselves to our inventory docs and we're just going to append a new ice and Stolley is to the image. Sorry. OK so now this is going to be an additional function only available to make play a carriage but not to my game character. If I try to call upon me to scroll down here. Need to go down if I try to call on my new game character darts and inventory I assume doesn't exist whereas mine you play a character don't add inventory if it does exist. So I can call on this I can pass and something like maybe our cards picked up like an X or something. And so if we would print out the inventory an X would be added to that. Now the Farnow concept so I want to show you is kind of method overriding in Python and this is the ability to take an existing method from our superclass and change its implementation very slightly. So I'm going to do this with change hit points because I now have these life attributes. So basically when I change my hit points to 0 I'm going to subtract one from the lives and then I'm going to change my current hit points back to 100. I'm not going to deal with the code that will delete the character if the current hit put 0 because something like some random animal that's running along the map there will be a non play character and when that hit points reach zero at that play that Karatz is probably going to die and disappear from the game or play character should do the same when our lives reach zero. So when our current hit points to 0 we'll subtract one from the lies when the lights are zero. We'd remove it from the game but we're not going to implement that code. We're just going to do the subtraction of our lives. So that means I want this. I want the same function because I still want to restrict my values but I want to provide additional functionality to it. Now that would be cool. Methadose writing and the way we go about doing this is like calling us by the same name. This function is here. So death changes hit points and I can go about doing this two ways. I can provide a completely different implementation if I want. All I can do is call on my superclusters implementation to execute this code and then provide additional code and I'm going to do the second option because I don't really want to repeat myself. So I'm going to call on my Super K dots. Oh actually it needs a put in these brackets just like we did up above. So we're gonna go super. Play character comma cells. Now if we call dots then we change our current hit points. So I'm just going to put the change and hit points in here. Now before we go ahead and change anything I'm just going to go ahead and make a call to change hit points and then run this so I call my new Actually let me let me zoom in make easy futureit I cool new play character talk change hit points and I'm just going to subtract safety from my current hit points and prints out of Avali this currently holds. So let's go here again and delete those other prints. OK so if I run this then I get 100 printed out because we started with an initial 150 and were subtracting 50 from it. The same could be said for our game characters so if we took a new game character and we were to change hit points again and change reports points just go subtract 50 from there and print outs print new game character dots. Current hit points so we have 50 or 100 because we start at 100 subtract 50 and so the second one we started at 150 and just subtracted 50 again. But now I'm going to provide a slightly different implementation for this and that's going to be to subtract one from our lives. OK so maybe to help demonstrate this point. Actually it would be easier if I added a Lives variable to this so I'm just going to add lives to my game character and then just apply the self-styled lives he equals you know I'm not going to set up in the initialiser that's going to cause problems later on. I was going to set up to be one right now here. So we'll start off with three Losar play Curtis one for just a regular game character. So now what I'm going to do it might change hit points is I'm going to make a call to this and then I'm going to say if our cells Dot's current hit points is less than or equal to zero and it shouldn't be less then because we've called on this we are simply going to take self-taught lives minus he calls 1 and then we can make the change in here. So if the cell dog lives is less then it is less than zero. We could just say something like self-taught lives self-taught lives equals zero. And that should be good to go. So also if we also try someone from our lives we simply want to change our self-taught car and hit points then back to maximum hit points. So self-taught max hit points just so that we can kind of reset that value. So we have a lot more going on in our change hit points we're dealing with subtracting one from our lives. But keep in mind this is actually only an hour of play character class. This implementation does not exist in our subclause in our superclass. So now let's see what happens when I call my change.

```python
    inventory = []
    def __init__(self, name, maxHP, xPos):
        super(PlayerCharacter, self).__init__(name, maxHP, xPos)
        self.lives = 3
        self.inventory = ["shirt","pants"]

    def addInventoryItem(self, newItem):
        self.inventory.append(newItem)

    def changeHP(self,changeInHP):
        super(PlayerCharacter, self).changeHP(changeInHP)
        if self.currentHP <= 0:
            self.lives -= 1
            if self.lives < 0

newGameCharacter = GameCharacter("Nimish",100,1)
newGameCharacter.changeHP(-50)
```

Hit points for both my player character and my game character and then print out the number of lives these characters have. So I'm just going to print my new game character daughter lives. And in here I'm going to print my and you play a character in adult life. And if I go ahead and run this then note that this certainly isn't enough to change our lives so let's just subtract let's say 200 from this and 200 and this will be more than enough. So if we go ahead and run this note that my numbers life's here is not changing and my current hit points is actually still zero. But here my current hit points have reset to 150 and I've subtracted one from my number of lives. So this means that we're still calling on our superclasses implementation here when we call on super play carriage change hit points but we're providing additional behavior that doesn't exist in the superclasses implementation. OK so this is called methadose writing and it's just a way to take an existing function in our superclass and change implementation slightly in the subclause. Now additionally if I wanted to go through all the work I could actually just have copied this and pasted it in and have ignored the super but why bother when I can just write this one line of code and ignore having to write these extra four or five. With that being said, that just about concludes our discussion on classes in Python. So we started by just Crace taught actually first about what classes and objects also remember objects, all the real kind of representation of a particular real world object they have state and behavior and the classes are just going off the code representation or the blueprints for a particular object. Objects and classes have proxies and behaviors proxies are defined with these variables up at the top here. Behavior is defined by these methods. Now we use initializations like this to create new instances of a class that are thought of as objects and contain some values for all of these properties and also we can act and we can execute these behaviors on those instances as well. We went over the concept of inheritance which provided a way for a subclass to inherit everything from supercluster. Note that my subclass here has all of these attributes without having to redefine them. But also we can define stuff of our own. So we overrode the initializer here and we also overload the extra function by calling on the superclasses implementation and providing a slightly different implementation as well. So these are just a couple of new instances we passed in the values because we specify what we need in the initializers and then just saw the example of the method overwriting down here. You access the functions classes or the classes functions and properties by calling on the instance name Dot's proxy name or top method name and you can also modify those properties as well. Assuming that these are not private and declare variables as private by adding two underscores in fronts, declare them as a turtle by adding just the one unschool. But as much as possible we want to kind of restrict or not restrict the access. So unless completely necessary. Avoid the use of the single and double underscores in front of these variables. One last thing I'll leave you with is a very very very brief discussion into polymorphism. So polymorphism is important in objects or in the program and basically states that well overall in application to our example it would be the case that our new play a character is an instance of game character and play a character which means it has everything game character has as well as everything that play a character has. Whereas a game character is not an instance of play, a character like a game character has everything that it has. But not everything that a character plays has. OK but with that being said we can just about conclude not only our discussion of classes and objects but our entire tutorial series on the Python language basics. So we start off learning Well first how to install Python and Python them towards a little bit about the I-T pie. The charm itself is how to create new files, how to find the stuff we need to and then how to compile and run our projects. Then we took a look at simple variables in Python that were the two main single variable types. The numbers and strings we took a look at multivariable types which were out arrays tuples and dictionaries that we explored control flow we talked about if statements else. If all else is an n I statement that we talked about our while and for loops then moved to functions and finally finished up without discussion on classes which is what we talked about here. So I know things weren't kind of quickly and didn't go too in-depth into a lot of these topics. Still honestly a lot I wanted to discuss but I'm trying to just give you the basics as quickly as I could and get you out there and ready to develop some actual programs of your own. So we'll probably be starting out with some of the basic tenso flow stuff. I think we'll be using pite charms for this as well. And if there's any new concepts that I haven't covered in this Python tutorial I'll introduce those at the time in which we cover them but otherwise the best way to learn more about Python is going to be to practice your own explore some of the options available to you as well as check online for look at. Like Stuff like the Python documentation itself. But that being said you should know enough from these five tutorial sections Zollo site the install and everything to get you started by developing some Python programs. It's really quite a fantastic language to use. I actually really enjoy using Python. It's so versatile so flexible and has such a huge number of applications so that being said will wrap this up. Thanks very much for setting up this tutorial again. I really appreciate the support and I speak not only on behalf of myself but on behalf of everyone here at Mammoth as well. So let's go ahead and get started by developing some actual Python programs. I think starting with a basic intro into tens of flow using Pocho.

EXAMPLE CODE

Classes in Python

Classes are a fundamental concept in object-oriented programming (OOP). They act as blueprints for creating objects that share similar properties (attributes) and behaviors (methods). Here's an example:

Python
```
class Car:
  """A simple Car class."""
  def __init__(self, make, model, year):
    """Initializes the car with attributes."""
    self.make = make
    self.model = model
    self.year = year

  define accelerate(self):
    """Simulates accelerating the car."""
    print(f"The {self.make} {self.model} is accelerating!")

# Create an object (instance) of the Car class
my_car = Car("Honda", "Civic", 2023)

# Access car attributes
print(f"Make: {my_car.make}")

# Call car methods
my_car.accelerate()
```

Use code with caution.

Explanation:

We define a class named Car with an __init__ method (constructor) that initializes attributes like make, model, and year when creating a new car object.

We define an accelerate method that prints a message.

We create an object (instance) of the Car class named my_car with specific values for its attributes.

We access attributes of my_car using dot notation (.) and call its accelerate method.

Wrap Up

This covers some basic concepts in Python:

Variables: Store data of different types (numbers, text, booleans, etc.).

Control Flow: Guide the program execution using if, for, while, loops etc.

Functions: Reusable blocks of code that perform specific tasks.

Classes: Blueprints for creating objects with attributes and methods.

Remember, this is just an introduction. As you explore Python further, you'll encounter more advanced functionalities within these concepts!

SETTING UP TENSORFLOW

What is up everyone and welcome to the first tutorial in our tents of flow series. My name is Nimish and with mammoth interactive and I'm going to be guiding you through this tutorial as well as through the next few tests close tutorials where we'll build a few projects together and we'll also show you how to add tens of flow to Android studio. Now at this point actually before we go any further I'm going to assume that you know at least a little bit about Python programming as well we're going to be working in pite shawm just because I think this is a nice idea and makes building and running our Python programs easy. So if you have no experience programming in Python or using Piko I suggest you watch your Tauriel series on the intro to Python in Python. I also did that one and should be included in the helo coding package anyway. But assuming you're comfortable enough with that stuff let's learn about tenses flow itself. So in this tutorial we're just going to be covering the basics. All also tend to flow components and roughly how to build a small program and use tends to flow in Python. So we'll start just by learning about each of the components. Also building up a tenth of the project including building up the computational graphs and then training your program. And finally we'll cover how to test your program by building a small program ourselves which will basically simulate a simple linear regression type model. Now keep in mind as we go through this tutorial that this is just going to be an intro into the very basics of the tenses of flow. And as we work through the other projects we go and see a variety of different libraries that are going to be used at a bunch of different machine learning techniques. However this is a good place to start if you have no machine learning experience particularly if you've never used tens of flow before. So without further ado let's get started. I just started up an instance on Python. Keep in mind this is version 20 seventeen point two point three and I'm going to be using Python 3.6. So make sure you've got all of the latest stuff because this will help with the imports if you don't have the latest version. In this version of Python you might not have access to some of the libraries we're going to be using.

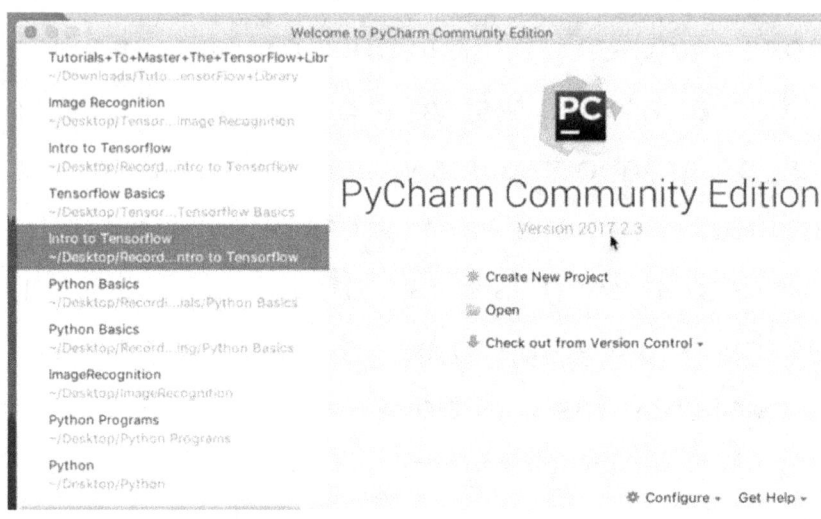

So we're just going to start by creating a new project. Let's just call this something like 10 so slow basic So in show you can actually instead of doing this click right on this item choose a location just like the desktop or something that's fine. Going to go ahead and open up. But make sure you're going to be saving this in a folder. You'll be able to easily access and probably won't be moving around too much. As you can see the search is going to be using three point six point two. And keep in mind if you use a different version of Python you might not have access to some of the same frameworks and libraries that we'll be using. So it will go out and create that project and don't worry about this we'll just go ahead and select no. And this just creates our new project for us. So it's just going to take a little while to get up . I just need to scan some files to index and then once that's done we'll start just with a basic intro. Insofar as what tends to flow is and what's going to do for us this is just going to be basically a text file that Iverson will just provide a brief intro into kind of the topics we're going to be covering as well as give an overview as to how tense the flow works and some of the components of it.

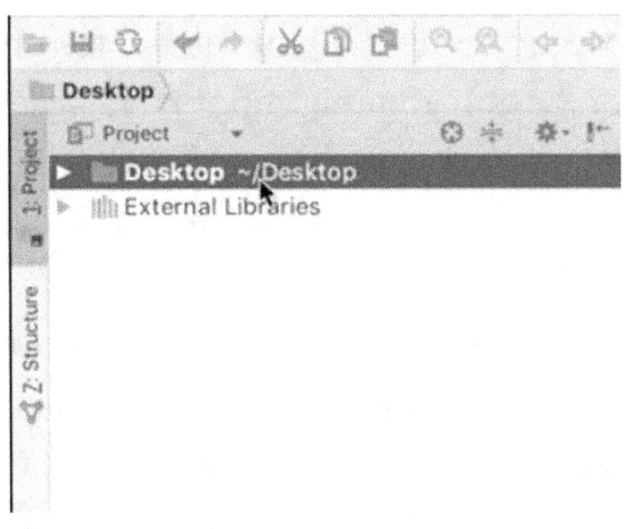

Once we're done with the intro We'll explore some specific components that we'll talk a little bit about linear regression then build up our linear regression model and then we'll be done and ready to start some type of real projects. So as always if you find that you are towards this will slow them, feel free to what she's a kind of one and a half or two time speed. But don't skip over entire sections as we're going to be covering some pretty complex stuff intensely. It can be a little confusing for those who have never used it before. So will we go ahead and get started with our brief talk into the overview of tenso flow and roughly how we're going to be using it in our projects?

EXAMPLE CODE

Here's an example of setting up TensorFlow in Python:

Python
```
import tensorflow as tf

# Print the TensorFlow version
print(f"TensorFlow version: {tf.__version__}")

# Create a simple constant tensor
hello_tensor = tf.constant("Hello, TensorFlow!")

# Print the tensor content
print(hello_tensor)

# Execute the operations defined above within a session
with tf.Session() as sess:
  # Evaluate the tensor and print the decoded string
  print(sess.run(hello_tensor))
```
Use code with caution.
Explanation:

Import the tensorflow library as tf.
Print the TensorFlow version.

Create a constant tensor named hello_tensor with the value "Hello, TensorFlow!".
Print the hello_tensor (which will show its details but not the actual value).
Create a session context using tf.Session(). This is typically needed for earlier versions of TensorFlow (before v2.0) but can still be used for code clarity.
Inside the session context, use sess.run to evaluate the hello_tensor and print the decoded string value.
Note: TensorFlow has recently undergone significant changes. While creating sessions was common practice, it's generally not required for newer versions. This example provides compatibility with both scenarios.

For more comprehensive setup instructions and advanced usage, refer to the official

TENSORFLOW INTRODUCTION

All right go is having Starseed out and you pile on projects and have gone over our learning goals. We can now launch into a quick discussion of exactly what tends to flow and how we might use it in our projects. Now this section is just designed as a brief overview off tends to flow as a whole not about the finer inner workings of it and it's just going to be basically a bunch of me talking and going over these points I've outlined here so if you already understand the basics of tensor flow feel free to skip this section but if you've never used tent's deploy before or you were a little unsure of how it works. I do encourage you to watch this. Now that being said you can watch with false ones as like I said it's just going to be basically a bunch of me talking and going over these points rather than writing any actual code. So let's go ahead and get started by talking exactly about what the tenets of flow are. So tons of flow is essentially a massive library that is used to incorporate machine learning into our projects. Now when I say that it's a massive library I mean that essentially it provides a bunch of high level API and data. So not only does it contain a bunch of variable functions and classes that will help us to build stuff like computation of graphs and run our actual models but it provides a bunch of already built in data sets or gives us easy access to those data sets. Now one of the great things about tenths of flow is that it can be incorporated into a large number of platforms. So we're just using it with Python and Pie Chaum right now but we can also incorporate it into stuff like mobile projects by imposing it into Android studio for example we're using it in web applications with Javascript. And unlike a lot of already included machine learning libraries and platforms it allows us to not only build and run our model but also to train the data ourselves at the same time these high level API is provide us a bunch of different again classes and functions that do a lot of the behind the scenes work for us. All we really need to do is build up our model and then go ahead and run it. That being said there's a few steps to this process which we'll explore in just a couple of minutes here. So the first tense of flow is built around the idea of tensors with no tenses or 10 songs on it.

Know how you want to pronounce them all base our basic units off data within tends to flow. So these we can essentially think of as being a race of primitive values such as arrays of strings, arrays of numbers and so on and so forth. This is how we're going to input our data into the model. Now that means that any kind of data that we're putting in bit images or audio or text or something like this. This all needs to be converted into tenso into arrays. This is easy enough. If we're just working with simple numerical models but for example stuff like a text prediction model might take in an array of text and we would have to divide that array of text. It's a small arrays of the individual strings that might represent single words. Similarly if with feeding and stuff like image data well then we need to convert the image data into basically these arrays or maybe pixel values all G.P.A. values or something like this. Either way the data we see didn't need to be in a text format. And this can be a lot of the challenge is trying to find a clever way to convert your data into a type into which we can feed or rather that we can feed into our model. Now as I just mentioned building a program intensive flow can be divided into two main sections or two main tasks. The first is going to be building up our computation of graph using nodes and a bunch of variables and values. And the second part is going to be running our craft, be it to train the model to assess the validity or accuracy of the model or to actually compute and predict something. So building the graph or the computational model it solves is in my opinion actually the hardest part about this. And the reason it's so difficult is that it's a pretty finicky process. There's a lot of different parameters to take into consideration. And finally the optimal model to use is prediction can be a bit Knauss in an office cell. This is unfortunately just something that comes with practice and experience using tends to flow. And the most optimal model is very often not clear right off the bat. However all I can do is teach you the basics, provide you with a few examples and then it's up to you guys to try to find the optimal solution to these problems. But the first step to building out a computational model or our computational graph and actually by the way as an aside when I say Graaff I don't mean kind of like an x and y axis kind of graph. I mean a graph that builds based on interconnected nodes. So if you're not sure what that is then search up something like a computer science graph and you'll get the general idea from there. So it was over saying our computational model is built entirely around a graph of nodes. So each of these nodes is going to take 0 or more tensors or a race as inputs. So again the first step is always going to be to convert our data that was feeding in into some kind of forum that will need to use various types of notes to build up our computational model as well will need to specify parameters such as the model type that we want to use. I think to keep things simple and because it's one of the simplest models anyway we're going to start off with a linear regression but we won't explore that in greater detail until a few seconds from now. We'll also want to specify stuff like a series of input parameters, input values and then the expected output that we'd get that would correspond with these. So for example let's say we had a building kind of like an image recognition model. Maybe that was a feat in some images like a boat, the cat in a rabbit or something and then the expected outputs would be the words that would represent those. So the inputs would be the images themselves obviously converted into intensive form and then the output would be the words that would represent those images as well. We'll need to specify which promises we want to optimize within our model. So for example with a simple linear regression model which is basically y equals x plus B the input values would be our x values the output values would be the y values and the promises we want our model to optimize would be our m or our slope and B which is y intercept. And then after this once we've built our model as basically across all nodes we'll probably want some kind of data to train our model as well as some data to test our model. Now generally speaking we want to divide our total dataset into about an 80 20 split. And I mean 80% said 20 percent. So 80 percent is going to be training data and 20 percent is going to be the testing data. Now the difference between the two is that the training data is obvious as its name might imply going to be used to train our model. So for example we'd feed in some images off again like a boat, a cat and a rabbit and we want to train our model in such a way that it will output those values then we'll of course want some testing data which is different from our training data. And this is going to be used to assess how accurate our role model is. So if at the end of the day our model is very inaccurate. We might want to either adjust the model promises or speed in some more data and train it further. So as you can see there's a lot that goes into building this model and there's a lot that can change about it which is why building this model can be so difficult. Sometimes you want a model that's not just accurate but also efficient as well. I mean if your model takes ages and ages days weeks maybe even months to process some data and give you a result probably not the best model and you'll probably want to either adjust the data set in cement oil once with just some of the promises as well as finding stuff like how to store our bottle as in the beginning values that we put in can be a challenge as well as typically will provide some initial values to these premises and then allow our model to adjust these values to find the optimal solution. However it's kind of difficult to understand how much of a challenge this can be without seeing the actual model right in front of us. As a quick example. So we'll save a further discussion for this when it comes time to actually start building up our simple linear regression model. So that's the basics of building up our models so once we have the model built the second step will be to obviously run our model. Now what I want to do this in a few different stages and the first stage will be to train our model so once we've trained it we'll run it on some testing data and then once we've done that and we're happy with the results we think our model is accurate enough then we can go to put some real data and go about using our model in the real world. So basically once the graph is built we run what's called a session on our graph and that will output any expected results or how accurate the model is, what the expected values are and so on and so forth. Now when we run it obviously will need some kind of input values to start off with and some kind of expected outputs. Now this is mostly used in our training data whereas when we're going to test it we'd simply just put in the inputs and then it would give us some outputs and we assess the validity accuracy of those results as well we'll want to specify how many Polk's we want to run as a model on which is essentially how many times we want the whole model to run. And also ones US specify stuff like the learning rates which is kind of how values are going to change over time and how quickly they will change again. This is a bit of an art in and of itself because if we run the model too many times it's just going to take too long to calculate the data. But if we don't run it enough times then we're probably not going to get accurate results. This is similar to trying to find the optimal learning rate because if we learn too slowly it's going to take ages and ages to run again. If we learn too quickly then we might get a slightly less accurate model. So although it's not difficult to use tens of, it actually makes things really easy again by providing these high level API. The challenge comes in finding the most efficient way to go about using it to solve your problems as well as finding enough a four hour training and testing datasets can be a bit of a problem particularly if you are using stuff like images. Luckily there are massive libraries out there some of which we gain access to thanks to trends and huge datasets that already allow us access to a bunch of already trained data or if we're building something completely new novel then we have to train the data ourselves. So although building the model can be the toughest part, training the model depending on how much data you are using can be the most time consuming part. But I'm not giving you all these warnings to kind of scare you away from this quite the opposite. I hope to treat you guys and get you guys thinking about how you might go about building your models, how you might go about training them in keeping all of these ideas in mind as we go to build our models to hopefully solve some interesting problems. And speaking of the models I'm actually at this point going to assume that you know at least some of the basics about some of the simple machine learning models that we might use. Now we're going to cover mostly linear regression. We may move into some of the other ones depending on how much time we have. But if you completely unsure and know nothing about machine learning and once know a bit more about some of the mechanisms behind some of these machine learning models I do recommend that you go and search for yourself as these tutorials are more about how to use tends to flow and incorporate it into your programs than about machine learning as a whole. Now that being said I will explain a bit more about linear regression. In a few sections when it comes time to actually build a simple linear regression model. So now just think about it as being basically a way to estimate a line that fits some data. Okay. And then we're going to run our model to basically optimize this fit. So essentially what this will do is again like I said linear regression is just using our basic question for line y m x plus B and then trying to find the optimal values for the slope and the intercept.

```
Tensorflow:

    - Tensorflow is a library used to incorporate machine learning into pro
    - Tensors are basic units of data and are arrays of primitive values
    - Programs have 2 sections: building graph with nodes, and running the
    - Building:
        - Build a graph of nodes, each takes 0+ tensors as input
        - Specify model type, input parameters, expected output, and parame
        - Might also want some training data and some testing data
    - Running:
        - Run the session on our graph to output any results
        - Specify how many times we want our model to run
        - First train with training data then use testing data to assess ac
    - One of the simplest models is linear regression. We basically estimat
        until the line adjusts to best fit the data, but more on this later
```

And this will help us to determine a line that best fits some data. So that's really what it does. It basically we see it in the inputs and the expected outputs and it trains this line to kind of move around until it finds that model that minimizes the differences between the X. The expectations and what's actually being outputted. But like I said more on this a little later in a few sections once we cover the very basics of how to build up our model will actually build a model from scratch ourselves but before we can do that we need to learn the code portion of how to build our computational model and we'll get started by learning about some nodes. So that's what's going to be coming up in this section. We'll just cover the basics of some of the nodes we might use and then either the next section or the one after that we'll talk about how to actually run our model to output the results found from building this computational graph. So hopefully by this point you understand a little bit more about exactly what you're going to be working with. And if you're happy and ready to move on. Let's start writing some actual code and starting to build up our computational growth.

CONSTANT AND OPERATION NODES

You guys at this point we know at least a little bit about how tens of floods work either from having watched out over the U.S. which we did previously or from just having some general knowledge of tents close to begin with. Either way we're going to start learning how to create our computational Grosch which will be essentially designing the model for our particular program. Now before we go about building the graph itself we need to learn about all of its components and how they work together with the simplest components of the graphs. I'll go and see our nodes. So we're going to explore all the different kinds of nodes that we'll be using to build our linear regression model starting in this section with our constants and our operation nodes. Now these are two of the most simple types and either hold a value or values or the results of some kind of an operation. So first take a look at how to set up and use these particular nodes. And we'll take a look at how to run the notes to output values using some tenths of flow sessions as the tutorial progresses and as we move on to the next few sections we can explore some different kinds of nodes. And then finally once we're comfortable with all of the nodes we'll be using in our leading regression model we can work to actually build up that model from the start. So let's work on our constant operation nodes. And before we can do anything else with tensor flow we have to import the tens of flow library. So this is done with a simple import statement. By the way I just started a new file here called this one node type part 1 and it just exists within my main directory right next to my notes here. So I think we can actually go ahead and close that project up and continue on with our import statements so we want to import tens of flow Okay. And I'm going to import this as T.F. so I can use my shorthand. Now unless you've already imported and installed tens of floats before this will likely give you a red squiggly line saying that you need to install the package. So you mean that you are using the latest version of pite charm and the latest version of python and know a little bit about Python programming and from previous experience or having watched our introductory Python tutorial then you should actually have access to this 10 supply package. So you just need to go ahead and install it. You can click on the 10th slot that sells the hold down option, press ENTER or turn and you should have as one of these options the ability to install tens of flow or to import the package. Now once you install it once it should be available for all your projects. Hence why I do not get an error. So I'm going to assume that from this point on you have successfully installed the. tends to flow and has access to all of its libraries. So just take a moment to go ahead and do that. You should only take about a minute to install the package and then come back to the section. So we're posting as T.F. just so we can use shorthand dots to gain access to all my library functions classes et cetera rather than having to type out to flow. So let's first explore constant nodes now for civil war cancer nodes. They're essentially a way to store a specific constant value within a particular node which we can then use to perform operations we can retrieve that value. And we actually can't do that much with it. It's just really a way to store that one value or multiple values in the form of an array. So we can create a constant node and store it within a variable just like we would any other Python variable. So I'm going to call this one constant Node 1 and it is going to set the sequence of Ts dot constants and this will give us access to a constant node. Now if you're not, the Lessel dialog window comes up and prompts us to enter a value, a type which is a data type, and we can answer to shape a name and this verify shape option which takes the true false value. You are only going to pass into these premises and only actually one is necessary. We just want the value because the data type is going to be implied from that. But I'm going to answer it anyway. So for a value we'll start with something simple like 1.000. So my value is one and if one I can answer a data type to be something like T.F. topflight those two. And we're going to be working a lot with Sloat, too. The reason being that we don't need the float Sixty-Four just takes up a little bit of extra space and we want floats because we want access to decimal values rather than just whole numbers. Alternatively I could actually make a constant two and I could do something else let's say 2.00 and I could completely forgo the day's type. And this is actually a perfectly valid constant note too. So once a constant note is a sign of value as we can see here it maintains that value throughout the duration of the program and cannot change hence it being a constant. Now if we were to print out this node right now however we wouldn't get any value associated with it. Although a node will have been created it will not store the value of 1 or 2 because we haven't actually created a session and run that session. So in order to actually give these constant nodes a value we have to run the session and that goes with any type of node. In fact all variable nodes will require an additional step but we'll get to those later on. So let's just print out these node values just to show you exactly what I mean. So I'll print out my constant Node 1 and I'm just going to copy this here prince again and we're going to do that no. 2. So if you start a new file as always I give this a save make sure when you go to run this you select your second option here. And in this case this is name or file node types. Part one you probably won't gain access to these these are for some reason popping up even though they actually exist in different projects. So as you can see they get to tensest being printed out here. There's no particular shape to these data types that float those two even though for the second one I didn't explicitly say so inferred that from the variable here. Now I could also see that these constants have no value associated with them. They're just storing the value of 0 right now. Again this is because we haven't actually run our session. So if we want to print out these values we could just call something like this. We would say the session equals our Ts dot session. So capsule S. Let me just zoom in that for you guys and we're just going to initialize it with an empty initialiser. Next we'll say session. Don't run. And then we want to feed in the values that we want in this case. I'm actually going to create an array or a tense as I should use the correct terminology and I'm just going to feed in my constant node one on my constant Node 2 at the end. I'm not going to print out these two nodes anymore because that's not going to return the same value as before. But instead I'm going to print out the results of the session run which will return a value which we could then store in a very bold print that we could just print the results directly. So if I go to run this you'll give me a bunch of warnings. You know what, don't worry about these warnings. They are just that they're not actually errors and it's just saying that this could go faster if we weren't working through python essentially But Python is a nice idea to work with. So we're going to continue to do so if you really want to suppress these warnings. I'll show you how to do that and allow some code at the very end that will help suppress these. Otherwise if we look at the actual values that were printed out as you can see we get the tenths of 1 and two. And that's because our first node had the value of one and now the second has the value of two. Now similarly if we had run each of these individually so let's get these out of the brackets here. And I'm going to run one at a time so copy this and paste it. This time I will do two. Then you can see it will get 1 and 2 being printed out one on top of the other just like this. Now right now we're storing single values. We can only store a tensor so we could have for example constant Node 3 be a constant. Now we can enter some kind of array here. I could do something like three point four point and I can even do another one by point or if I really wanted then if I was a prince out the value of my constant note after of course I run it then it's going to print out this tensor here.

```python
# Explore constant and operator nodes
# How to set up and use nodes
# How to run nodes to output their values

import tensorflow as tf

const_node_1 = tf.constant(1.0, dtype=tf.float32)
const_node_2 = tf.constant(2.0)
const_node_3 = tf.constant([3.0, 4.0, 5.0])

session = tf.Session()
print(session.run(const_node_1))
print(session.run(const_node_2))
```

Now where possible we should probably specify a data type so I'm going to go ahead and add that to each of these. They're all going to be float 32. So we can actually just copy that and paste it right in there. So when I set the time to be like 32 that implies that every single one of these values within the tensor here will be like 32 also. Now the reason we've got nothing printed out before is because again we haven't run these nodes. And so none of the values stored at these nodes is going to be evaluated; it's only once we call them the session and run that particular note that the value at that node is evaluated. So anything goes for even notes that feed into other nodes. If none of the nodes are running then we're not going to get any values printed out because none of the nodes will be evaluated. However we have a node for example one of these operating nodes whose value depends on other nodes and then we run that operate a node then essentially it's going to run all of the other connected nodes as well or at least the ones that feed into it's not necessarily the ones it feeds into. So for example let me just create a couple of operation nodes. So we'll start over with the basic addition. And the stories in any other variable just like we with these constant nodes. Instead of calling TSTO constants we can call something like this. I'm going to call this at node 1 and it's going to be TS dots and note that this is one of the operations just like if we were to do something like T.F. dot multiply and so on and so forth. In this case I'm just going to do a T.F. to add and which simply goes to two notes that we want to add. In this case are just two constant one and constant two. So if I were to run now add a note instead. So I'm just going to get rid of the second print statement and now instead of running constant no one will ever run out of node one. So it's just a mountain to give us a run. We should get the results of the addition that way. So that being printed and we do 3.00. Additionally we actually don't have to create don't use a special type of node. We could do something like this on a node one equals just something like constant node 1 plus constant node 2. And then if we have to run this we would achieve as many exactly the same insects as possible. You know what the results are in something different just so that we can see that contrast. So for us to run again should be exactly the same again. 3.00 it is being printed out. Let's say for example that we had another operation being performed. So let's say we want to multiply something this time so we can either create a separate TSTO multiply node or we can simply call on the operation one of these nodes times one of the others. We'll just keep things simple. I'm going to call this Moltz node 1. So I must play node 1 and we're just going to set this equal to the results of added to multiplied by every element within this tensor here. So we can just call on something like add a node 2 times constant Node 3. So what this will do and if you understand any kind of matrix multiplication is it will take each of these elements and all multiply them by the results of this addition. So that's going to return us three times three so it should be 9, 12 and 15. If we were to run a multi node one system out could this have run at sea we do get that 9 12 and 15 it exactly what we should expect. But this is run on multi node one which means that it's not only running multi node one it has to run out at node 2 and it has to run constant Node 3. And now I don't know if cells have to run Consta Node 1 and Constant Node 2. So essentially we get 1 2 3 4 5. No, it's being run in total. However if we were to run in this case out an or two but not multi Node 1 then this is not going to perform this operation so multi node one is just not going to be run at all it will only run at a node 2 and then that will in turn pro and con. Node 1 and 2. So pretty straightforward stuff here. We can also deal with two antennas if we want so if I want to create Konst a node for the hardest sulfur tensor then then perform some operations. For example adding each of the elements together or adding one of these to each of these elements or something like that. That's a perfectly valid operation to perform as well. So even the results of an operation like this will be stored within the node itself. So we are essentially building a power graph piece by piece by including all of these operations and these constant nodes now constant nodes are obviously very inflexible in that they can only hold the one value or multiple values and that value can't change which means they are not particularly good for use in the computers a sense of trying to change variable values or for input values because of course we want to be able to at some point take an input from the user or have the computer multiply these values to predict the model successfully.

```
import tensorflow as tf

const_node_1 = tf.constant(1.0, dtype=tf.float32)
const_node_2 = tf.constant(2.0, dtype=tf.float32)
const_node_3 = tf.constant([3.0, 4.0, 5.0], dtype=tf.float32)

adder_node_1 = tf.add(const_node_1, const_node_2)
adder_node_2 = const_node_1 + const_node_2
mult_node_1 = adder_node_2 * const_node_3

session = tf.Session()
print(session.run(mult_node_1))
```

So use these constant nodes whenever you want. Well a Constans the operation nodes however will continue to continue to be used throughout very often. But if we want something a little more flexible to work with we're going to have to introduce either a placeholder or variable nodes. So let's take a look first at placeholder nodes and then we'll move on. I think we'll do separate sections to that too. So in the section Coming up we'll take a look at placeholders and then the section afterwards we can take a look at how variable nodes then once we have finished with variable nodes that we can start to actually build up our model beginning with the basic intro to the linear regression model we're going to be using. So unless you're totally 100 percent comfortable , play around with it a little bit. And once you are ready to move on, move on to the next section which will introduce the placeholder node.

EXAMPLE CODE

```python
Python
import tensorflow as tf

# Create a constant node with numeric value
const_1 = tf.constant(5.0, name="Input_1")  # Name for clarity

# Define an operation node for addition
add_op = tf.add(const_1, 10, name="Add")  # Operation and name

# Print the nodes created in the TensorFlow graph (not executed yet)
print(f"Constant Node: {const_1.name}")
print(f"Operation Node: {add_op.name}")

# Start a session (optional for newer TensorFlow versions)
with tf.Session() as sess:
  # Run the operations and get the result
  result = sess.run(add_op)

  # Print the final result
  print(f"Result of adding constant and value: {result}")
Use code with caution.
```

Explanation:

Import TensorFlow as tf.
Create a constant node named const_1 with the value 5.0. We assign a name "Input_1" for better understanding of the graph.
Define an operation node named add_op that performs addition between const_1 and the value 10. We also assign a name "Add" for clarity.
Print the names of the created nodes (const_1 and add_op). These exist in the TensorFlow graph but haven't been executed yet.
Create a session context with tf.Session() (optional for some TensorFlow versions).
Inside the session, use sess.run to execute the add_op and store the result.
Print the final result, which should be 15.0 (5.0 + 10).

Key Points:

tf.constant creates a constant tensor node.
tf.add defines an operation node for addition.
The code uses names for the nodes to improve readability when working with the TensorFlow graph.
Executing the operations happens within the session context (optional for some versions).

PLACEHOLDER NODES

Everyone having covered two out of four of how a simple no type so far we can now move onto the third which is going to be our placeholder node. So whereas with the constant nodes and actually the operation nodes as well were kind of assigning a value right away placeholder nodes actually contain no current value. When we create them it's only when we go to run the session and therefore run the nodes that we pass in some kind of a value to these nodes. So essentially when we build our cross up we are saying OK here is an empty Note that will contain a value but we just don't know what that value is going to be right now. So then when we go to run the entire graph then we need to pass on a value for each of these placeholder nodes if we want something to actually happen with it. So we can kind of think about these being nodes that would take in the input into our model. So thinking quickly back to our linear regression model like m x plus B and B you're going to be the variable nodes. Those are things that the model tries to optimize itself. But X would be a good place for a placeholder node because we need to pass in x values when we run the program. Similarly when we're testing the program or training it rather we'll probably want to Palsson some y values as well. So why would there be another place where we might add a placeholder node. But then of talking you guys came here to code so let's get to coding. The first thing we need to do is of course import tends to flow as he asked. And the reason that has to happen is because I'm starting a new file, this one I've called no types part 2. Whereas previously we would work in part one of actually included Part 1 here kind of close up open source new file which also means when I go to run the sky I'm going to have to run Of course my no type's part to make sure I'm in this file here. So nothing should really occur. We should have an MC run screen. I haven't told this guy to print anything yet. Once you install tens of flow once it should be forever installed in pide Sharma unless you go and deliberately delete it. So you shouldn't have to install it yet again. Just make sure you import. OK so we set a placeholder. No it's kind of similarly to how we'd set up a constant node except that we don't provide a value right away. We say we do store them in variables however. So I'm going to call this place hold the one place all the nodes one place all the One doesn't matter. I'm going to set the sequel to ts dolt's placeholder. It takes in a few promises so DS type shape and name. There's no value parameter here which makes sense. We don't want to pass in value right away. Now actually I'm going to give this guy right now is going to be a D type so D type equals TFT or Sloat 32 as usual and I'm not going to worry about the shape or anything. Actually you know what I probably should have explained in the previous section. I might as well get into this now. So let me talk about the shape of a tense. And that's what I was referring to. We talk about basically the degree as the array or how many arrays there are within that particular array. So consider this literal and primitive number 5.0. Well this has a shape of 0 or the shape doesn't exist. Ok this is because first of all this isn't in a tensor. And second of all there are no tenses within tenses right. However if I were to put this in a tensor like this suddenly my shape takes on this value so this would be 00 my shape now equals something like 1 0. OK this is because there is one. Actually rather than 0 0 These actually are just blank and blank because the shape doesn't really apply here. Well in this case this is actually just going to be one blank because there is one member within this array within this tensor. But there are no additional arrays, there are no tenses to take on additional shapes. If we went one step further and had something like this an array within an array 5.0 like this then our shape all of a sudden becomes 1 and 1. The reason being there is one array within our array and there is one member within the array. Hence one also one in array and one member within the array. So we could then add some variations here if we had a couple of arrays Perhaps each with just a memo with just one member here. So 5.0 and then like 1.0 or something. Well in this case my shape is 2 and 1 because too many or two in arrays each with only one member. And so if each of these had a couple of members as well so for point this one could maybe be two points. Then in this case my shape becomes 2 because again to raise each with two members this time and so on and so forth. So this is you. This is the basics of how it tends to shape and that's just what it means but it's clearly something that we don't have to specify seeing as we are able to assign the variable. No problem just for the sake of demonstration. I'm actually going to add in a placeholder too. Which is also going to be a float does he too. Now if I were to print these right now I haven't created a session yet so we would get basically just some empty tenses. But if I were to create a session so same as before which is going to say session equals t as session is a good idea actually to keep typing this out. Just see you get in the habit and it becomes second nature. You don't have to think about it. We could say the session doesn't run and we're actually going to print the results. So let's just go to the end and let's say I were to print my placeholder one rather than just entering and placeholder one like we would have done with the constants we have to provide a value to this as well. So not only am I going to run a placeholder one but I'm going to provide some values too so I have to answer the code here.

```python
# Placeholder nodes
# Nodes with no current value
# Pass in value when running session

import tensorflow as tf

placeholder_1 = tf.placeholder(dtype=tf.float32)
placeholder_2 = tf.placeholder(dtype=tf.float32)

session = tf.Session()
print(session.run(placeholder_1))
```

And then afterwards provide some values I could answer just a single value like this. Or you could enter a tensor with a few values. So let's just mix things up, let's answer tensor to point. We can do it. Why not? Point I was well. Was giving me an error right now because we need to place these in curly braces like this. OK so if we were to go ahead and run this now we're printing out the result so let's give it a whirl and let's see what gets output here. We're getting a massive amount of errors. I think I see what the issue is. Forgot to add a placeholder one here. I need to pass in the values when I go to run it. So there we go to fix the issue. We need to make sure we're running the node itself and then we're entering some values for it. So that's what was as you can get the array 1 2 and 3 being printed out there. So we do exactly the same thing for placeholders too. And we do exactly the same thing if we wanted to enter in only a single family. So for example for point 0 going around that again we just get the value for prints at that. So essentially what this does is it assigns two placeholder one for this particular value or values if we enter the tensor and then it's going to run placeholder 1 with that particular value. Now we ran something like placeholder 1 with placeholder to contain this value. That's going to be particularly useful to us as you can see it gives us this massive error because it's saying we'll place the one still doesn't have a value we haven't assigned it here. So make sure any time you're going to run a placeholder node you need to provide a value for that. So it's important to keep track of all your placeholders as if you don't enter in values you get this ugly error here. But that being said we can actually perform some operations on placeholders. So we're going to take this one step further and create an operation node. So we'll just do a simple multiply operation. OK we'll call this multiple node and this is basically going to be the results of placeholder 1 Times place. Hold it. There we go. Now what we want to do is run multiple nodes. So I'm going to replace the note I'm going to run with multiply node and now I need to enter values not just the placeholder one but also it's a placeholder too because I'm going to be using both of these placeholders if for whatever reason I was only using one of these placeholders and I'd only need to answer the values for that. So actually before we do this let's just do we'll call this multiply node 2. And we're going to run miles, plain old ones which I'm just going to create right now. We'll sit in one there and want to hear this is just going to be something like a placeholder 1 times 3. And so if we wanted to run just multiply no one as you can see we're taking in a literal value and we're taking a placeholder node so we need to provide a value for the placeholder node. This will suffice for points. Oh. So let's go ahead and get this around and let's see what output we get. We get 12 so that's to be expected as 3 times 4 does in fact equal 12. But if we were to run multiply Node 2 we need to provide values for both placeholders 1 and 2. So it's run now and these provide a value here. And we need to provide a value for placeholders too. So in this case let's switch it up, let's make this a tensor. Will do 2.00. 2.0 and let's do a lawsuit 5.0 and Kafe doesn't really matter. It's entirely up to us. So now if we go to run this we should get our tenso here being multiplied appropriately.

```python
# Placeholder nodes
# Nodes with no current value
# Pass in value when running session

import tensorflow as tf

placeholder_1 = tf.placeholder(dtype=tf.float32)
placeholder_2 = tf.placeholder(dtype=tf.float32)

multiply_node_1 = placeholder_1 * 3
multiply_node_2 = placeholder_1 * placeholder_2

session = tf.Session()
print(session.run(multiply_node_2, {placeholder_1: 4.0, placeholder_2: [2.0, 5.0]}))
```

We are multiplying it by force of course two times four is 8 5 times 4 is 20. So we know this is working exactly as it should. Okay. So just to mount and review what we've done so far. So that's certainly the basics of placeholders are very straight forward and we just need to make sure that you are providing a value for them if you're going to use them at some point down the line even if there's a node connecting a node connecting node connecting a note that connects to a placeholder at some point because it's still connected to that placeholder. You do need to provide a value at some point. However if you're not going to be using a placeholder like we saw in the first case with placeholder to provide a value for it just doesn't make sense to do so. But as you can see when we run this we are entering in value so it's a very good place to enter an input. We can kind of think about them as being like function promises. All right. So placeholders are a good place for input. They are just a promise to hold some kind of value. Once they're assigned a value we can treat them just like we would a constant node. So with that being said we can conclude this part. Let's give that a save and we'll end the section. Moving on to the next part which is going to be Alwa variable notes and things are going to be kind of similar to constant nodes but obviously they can change hence the name variable. And there's actually going to be one extra step we need to take if we want to run them. I'll explain that later. Otherwise make sure you're comfortable with placeholder nodes before moving on as things are only going to get weirder from here on out. So let's go learn about some variable nodes for.

EXAMPLE CODE

```python
import tensorflow as tf

# Define a placeholder node for an unspecified numeric input
x = tf.placeholder(tf.float32, name="Input")  # Name for clarity

# Define an operation node for multiplication by 2
multiply_op = tf.multiply(x, 2, name="Multiply")  # Operation and name

# Start a session
with tf.Session() as sess:
  # Provide a value for the placeholder during execution (not defined before)
  input_value = 5.0

  # Run the operation with the provided value for the placeholder
```

```
  result = sess.run(multiply_op, feed_dict={x: input_value})

  # Print the final result
  print(f"Result of multiplying input by 2: {result}")
```
Use code with caution.

Explanation:

Import TensorFlow as tf.
Define a placeholder node named x with data type tf.float32. This acts like a placeholder for an input value that will be provided later. We assign a name "Input" for better understanding.
Define an operation node named multiply_op that performs multiplication between the placeholder x and the value 2. We also assign a name "Multiply" for clarity.
Create a session context with tf.Session().
Inside the session, define a variable input_value with the actual value (5.0 in this case). This value will be fed to the placeholder when running the operation.
Use sess.run to execute the multiply_op. However, this time, we also provide a feed_dict argument. This dictionary maps the placeholder (x) to the actual input value (input_value).
Print the final result, which should be 10.0 (5.0 *

2).
Key Points:

tf.placeholder creates a placeholder node that represents an unspecified input value.
You provide the actual value for the placeholder during execution using a feed_dict argument in sess.run.
Placeholder nodes allow for flexible input during runtime, making the computation more adaptable.

VARIABLE NODES

All right guys having explored three out of our four basic no types we can all move on to the fourth and final one which will be our variable nodes so variable knows initially start out like constant nodes and that we typically assign an initial value maybe a data type. But there's actually some pretty significant differences between variables and constant nodes. So the three main differences are the fact that although we store an initial value we can place it to change that value in a variable node whereas with a constant node we actually can't reassign any kind of value once the values are stored. The second big difference is that when we go to run a variable now to evaluate the value it holds we have to call upon and initialize it to first assign the value to all variables. We'll explore this process towards the end and the third difference is going to be the fact that our well variable nodes actually have a ton of attached extra functionality. So this means as a bunch of extra functions that we can call on on variable nodes there's a bunch of different values we can retrieve that aren't necessarily for our constant nodes. So let's jump right into some examples. I've just started a new file as you can see no types three this time.

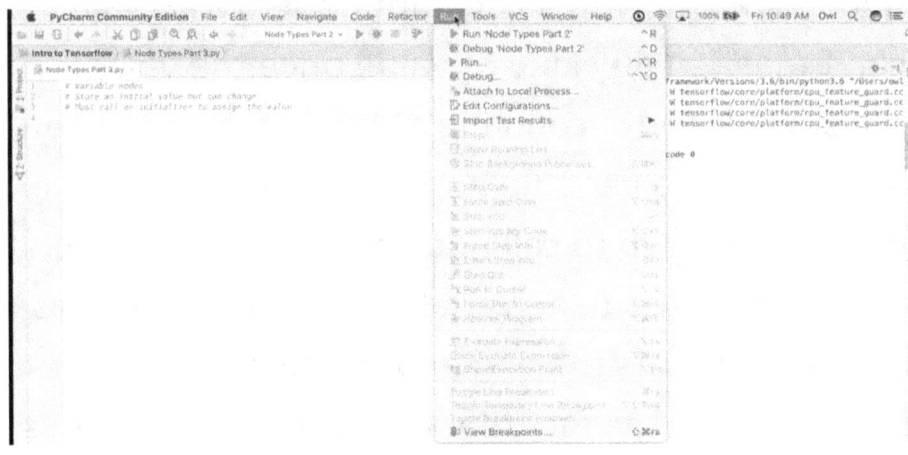

So when I go to run things I need to make sure that I'm running my correct file. In this case no types part three empty screen that's what I expect. So the first step is always going to be to import tens of flow if we want access to any of the tens of Flo's stuff. So we're going to import tens of flowers as he asks. And now we can start by creating some variable nodes. So start with just the one for now terrible Node 1 and get a second sequel to Ts dot variable capsule's. Because this is a class or. Well we're actually creating an instance of the class and we open up our bracket. Say you'll note there's a ton of different problems as we can answer it. So already you can see that all variables are quite a bit more complex on our constant nodes as a constant node only has a few options to choose from. Well because we're keeping things simple I'm going to pass in a simple value of like 5.0 or something and I might as well Palsson a data type just to make things as clear as I can. T.F. Das float Tousey two should do the trick. And for demonstration purposes imagine a Cray constant node as well. TSTO constant This should be pretty routine to you guys by now. I'll just fill in a value of 10 I can add in the data type as well if I really want to look again. And that's really all there is to setting up a basic variable node. So like I said it starts out looking very similar to a constant. The big difference that we see right off the bat is when we go to run these nodes. So whereas I could just create a session and set the sequel to TFT or session capsule again and then go ahead and run this one so I could print the session run and I could enter in my constant Node 1. I can absolutely do this. So if I go to run this one it's just going to print out the value found at my constant node 10.00 I can actually do this with my variable node. So if I replace my constant with a variable node book and try to run this, that is going to give me a bunch of errors. OK that's the problem here is that although we think we've assigned the value to the variable we haven't actually initialized it. So as of now this variable Node 1 actually doesn't hold this value and that's why it's making so many errors in order to have this take on value. We have to create a global initialiser. So let's call this in its. And this is just going to be our T.F. dot global variables initialiser and then we have to run our initialiser. So actually you know what I'm going to print this on this line Undenatured and then we're going to call on our session to run our initialiser and then we can run our prince statement. So now if we were to run this we should successfully get the value of our favorable note printed out and indeed we do. That's just going to be 5.0 Now this global variable initialized here this initializes all of our Ts dot variable nodes. So this means if I had say No. 2 and 3 and 4 and 5 I had a bunch of different variable nodes this cool to our global variables initialiser just once will initialize all of them. So typically we'll only ever have to call this one before we go to evaluate any values found at those nodes. Now again if there's going to be any other nodes that rely on our variable no node to have a value. So those are connected nodes leading into that that we have to call on our global variables initialized before we gain access to any of the values that have to do with our variable node. So if you have any variable nodes at all in your project always make sure you're calling on this initializer. Now we don't actually have to create a new variable. I could just have passed this line of code into my run statement here just trying to make things a little clearer for you guys. Now other than seeing as we've initialized our variable here that we can use it just like we would any other kind of node. So for example I can perform any kind of operation here , could multiply this by constant Node 1 and run it should give me 50. Indeed it does 10 times five is 50 and I can perform a large number of other operations on these guys. So right off the bat when I start typing out my say Canzano 1 don't note that there's really not a lot I can choose from. However if I call upon my variable node then there's a ton of different functions and values I can retrieve. And the fact that the mass probably stems from our variable being a class, which is constant, is just non-class; you can tell that both from the capsule lessa here and from the fact a cycle variable. Let's say if I call TFK a variable is a class here whereas FDR constant does not provide us a class is just a function. So something we might want to do with variable nodes because you know what. Otherwise why not use just a simple concept. It's going to be to reassign the value. Now all I need to do really is call upon my variable Node 1 dots assign and then enter it and you Gallia in this case maybe I want to ensure the value of 10 not doing this itself is not quite enough. We have to actually run this just like we would run something like this to evaluate the node or run our initialiser. So if I were to assign the values 10 and then run it like this. Well nothing's going to happen. In fact let me demonstrate that. Let me just print out a session to run and I'm just going to print out the new value of variable Node 1 or so I might think so if I go to run this but I get 5 printed out there so clearly this re-assignment hasn't worked.

```python
# Variable nodes
# Store an initial value but can change
# Must call an initializer to assign the value

import tensorflow as tf

var_node_1 = tf.Variable([5.0], dtype=tf.float32)
const_node_1 = tf.constant([10.0], dtype=tf.float32)

session = tf.Session()
init = tf.global_variables_initializer()
session.run(init)
print(session.run(var_node_1 * const_node_1))

session.run(var_node_1.assign([10.0]))
print(session.run(var_node_1))
```

Well like I said before we're going to have to run this in our session just like we would have done otherwise and now it can take on the value of 10 so if we go to run against get a print out of 50 and then is printing out 10 because we've successfully reassigned it's value down the other not that is pretty much the basics of our variable type nodes. Now like I said there's a ton of different stuff we can do with them. So I suggest playing around with it a bit before moving onto the next part. But at this point you know actually everything you need to know about for basic no types to start take a look at our linear regression model. Now I know we haven't covered each of these in huge depth. I could go much deeper into each of the topics. I just want to get you guys knowledgeable enough so that you can start work on the actual linear regression model and get into some interesting stuff because that's what we're going to be covering in the next couple of sections. That's really what I've been leading up towards. It's one Schaus familiar enough that we can successfully build up this model and get started with some real machine learning. So I think in the next section before we actually start building up the model which we'll do over the next few sections we're just going to start talking a little bit more about linear regression itself, how it's going to work and kind of go through the steps then we'll start actually writing the code. So once you are comfortable enough with variables, given them that little bit of practice and ready to move on, do so and we'll see you in the linear regression sections.

EXAMPLE CODE

Python

```python
import tensorflow as tf

# Define a variable node with an initial value
learning_rate = tf.Variable(0.1, name="Learning_Rate")  # Name for clarity

# Define an operation node for updating the variable
update_op = learning_rate.assign_add(0.01)  # Increment by 0.01

# Start a session
with tf.Session() as sess:
  # Initialize the variable before usage (important for variables)
  sess.run(tf.global_variables_initializer())

  # Print the initial value of the variable
  print(f"Initial learning rate: {sess.run(learning_rate)}")

  # Run the update operation a few times
  for _ in range(3):
    sess.run(update_op)

  # Print the updated value of the variable
  print(f"Learning rate after 3 updates: {sess.run(learning_rate)}")
```

Use code with caution.
Explanation:

Import TensorFlow as tf.
Define a variable node named learning_rate with an initial value of 0.1. We assign a name "Learning_Rate" for better understanding.
Define an operation node named update_op that updates the learning_rate variable using the assign_add method. This adds 0.01 to the current value.
Create a session context with tf.Session().
Inside the session, initialize all variables using tf.global_variables_initializer(). This is crucial for variables as they don't hold a value until explicitly initialized.
Print the initial value of the learning_rate variable using sess.run.
Use a loop to run the update_op three times, effectively updating the learning_rate variable in each iteration.
Print the updated value of the learning_rate variable again using sess.run.
Key Points:

tf.Variable creates a variable node that can store and update its value during training or computation.

> Variable nodes need to be initialized before use with tf.global_variables_initializer().
> Operations can be defined to modify the variable values (like update_op in this case).
> Variable nodes are essential for machine learning tasks where parameters are learned during training.

MAKING A LINEAR REGRESSION MODEL

Hi guys by this point we've learned some of the key components to building our computational graphs specifically we covered four different kinds of nodes. We're going to be using throws as well as how to create a session and then run it to evaluate how those node values will change. So with that in mind we know just about enough to start building up our actual computational model from the ground up before we start writing any code that represents the model itself. However I'm just going to take a few minutes to talk a little bit about linear regression which is going to be the model that we'll be using as well as give a brief overview as to the steps that we're going to be taking to build this model intensively slowly. So for those of you who are very familiar with linear regression particularly using it intensively then feel free to skip the section if you guys know nothing about linear regression or know some but not how to use an intensive flow then this might be a good place to start. OK so I'll try to keep it short and to the point. Now first of all why linear regression as opposed to any other machine learning model will in my opinion I think linear regression is probably one of the simplest machine learning models to simulate. And this is because it operates on the principle equation of a line which is just Wike was M-x plus b so typically once so a model already works just fine it will have adjusted M and B to provide some optimal values will simply be able to enter in some x inputs and it will outputs where the y values should be based on this line that will have been optimized by our program. And essentially this is a really good way to predict where points should lie on a line of best fit. So essentially we'll have a bunch of data points and we're trying to find a line of best fit through those points. We'll use our model to optimize and be until it finds that perfect line or as close to perfect as we can get. And once it finds that good lines then we'll have a complete model. So as I said it tries to adjust and be until it minimizes what we call loss. Now lost is the difference between an actual y value and the y value that a line would predict. So let's say we have some arbitrary line running through a set of data. Well the loss will be basically the sum of all the differences between the actual y points we get and the y points that run along the line itself. So by minimizing this overall loss value we're actually computing the line that best fits the data that has a minimal loss will basically imply that the points are as close to the line as they can get. Now if you want to learn more about the specifics about how linear regression works I do recommend that you do some research of your own. Otherwise it all sumed that you get the basic idea. And we're going to cover some of this stuff again. Anyway once we start writing the code we're going to go about doing this by first building our model and then training it. So we'll build the model up using a series of nodes some of them will be placeholders some of them will be variable some constants and we'll probably start with something like some placeholder nodes for our x and y values as we once take these both in as inputs. At the end of the model we'll be able to just take in the x values as inputs and housewifely uses outputs but at least in the training phase we want some extra values and they're expected y values so the wife always correspond with them in order to train our model at least then we'll probably have some variable modes to represent and B we'll just start out with some initial guesses and see how good or bad those guesses are by measuring our loss then essentially we'll create other nodes. And finally will run our program in the training phase that our program will basically adjust and be values to overall minimize the loss based on some kind of inputs that we enter. So after it's been sufficiently trained and has found optimal values for A and B will again be able to just enter in any kind of x value and it should give us Rastelli what the corresponding y values should be. And our final model will just provide a good fit line through our data and should be able to predict those white values. So the underlying concepts here are awfully simple but just given the fact that this might be an entirely new thing to use tends to flow and right machine learning programs.

```
Node Types Part 3

r Regression Points
  - Linear regression is one of the simplest machine learning models (y = mx + b)
  - Try to fit a line of best fit through some data points to help with prediction
  - Program optimizes line by adjusting m and b until it minimizes loss
     - loss is the difference between an actual y value and the line itself
     - minimal loss corresponds with a line that best fits the data as points are on average closer to the line
  - Training our model:
     - Take x values and expected y values as inputs
     - Start with guess for m and b and measure loss
     - Run program to adjust m and b to minimize loss based on inputs
  - Final model will fit a good line through data and will be able to predict correct y values given x input
```

It can be a somewhat complex process and is easy to get lost. So hopefully I understood some of this if you want to learn more about linear regression again and culchies do some research on your own. Otherwise I'll try to go slowly through the actual building of the computational model. Unexplained exactly what's going on at each step so that we're never lost. But as always, it's very important here. You need to understand the stuff that we are covering in the currents section as well as have covered in the previous sections before moving on to the next because like I said it is very easy to get lost along the way and there's like a couple of lines of code that don't really make sense right away. Otherwise with this brief incher done we are just about ready to start building up our computational model. As always we'll start by building the graphs that we'll start by and then we'll move on to training. And finally we'll use some test data to assess accuracy if I will model and we're going to do so in one or two different files so this one I just created a new text file for I guess I'll include this in the final product although again hopefully by the end you won't know it you won't need this as you'll be fairly familiar with the mechanisms. So let's go ahead and get started by building up our computational cross.

BUILDING A LINEAR REGRESSION MODEL

OK guys I think it's finally time for us to start writing some code that will eventually build up our linear regression model. Now we'll build up a useful model in three main phases. This one is going to be the first one in which we'll be just building up with computational graphs so we'll specify what kind of nodes we'll need. We'll create some variables and essentially build up the basics of our Grof. So the second part we'll deal with actually training our model to try to optimize those values for our slope and for our y intercept. And then finally the last part we'll be actually testing the accuracy of our model. So if you haven't already I would recommend you start either a new file or just common everything else from the previous stuff as I don't want any kind of variable interference. But otherwise we can close up this project. I've called my file linear regression model so I need like that from my run window and make sure that that's the one I'm going to be running from now on which it should just be a blank run screen for now. OK so we're going to begin as we always do by importing tens of flow that's going to be quite necessary to access everything we need and then let's start thinking about the model itself so we know we're going to be using linear regression like was M-x plus B. We know that X is going to take it. X is always going to take in some kind of input from the user. So probably a placeholder note for this. And as we train our model will lead to provide some expected y values so we'll also make a y placeholder node. Now m and b are going to be changed by the model itself. So these are probably going to be stored within some kind of variable nodes. Now very often you will actually see this W instead of M and this is just the kind of addicts that have a bunch of weights so you can call it WOSM whatever you want just to keep in line with the models that are devastated elsewhere and I tend to do slow documentation stuff. I'm just going to go with a W. instead of an atom. Now we don't have a bunch of data to work with. So let's just create some fake data right now. So that's punched in a bunch of x values we'll just do like one two three and four. And then we'll have some y values also that should correspond with these x values and the values we pick for y. Really it's entirely up to us but I'd recommend that you follow along with my values just to kind of keep things consistent until you understand fully how it works and he can answer your own values. I'm just going to actually do a negative slope off a negative slope. So we'll start with zero. We can do negative one, negative two and negative three. So if these were the expected at these with our inputs and these were the expected corresponding outputs it's pretty easy to see that our slope is just a negative one and our wife Ali is a positive one or are y intercept. But the computer doesn't know that and very often this is not going to be so easy to see. So what we'll do is we'll create a couple of variables that will wrap presents Alwa W and B. And we'll just fill them in with some kind of random guesses. Let's just pretend that we actually have no idea what the slope and what the Y in Sept should be. So we'll just put in some numbers and then try to optimize those results. So these will actually store in some nodes like I said we'll use variable nodes for WMP and probably some placeholder nodes for x and y. So we could just create a W. This is simply going to be the dots and we want some variable nodes for this. So then our variable node will pert I guess some kind of initial value and the data type will though again data type not necessary. This is just going to be a float too. And I'm actually just going to copy this and do the same for B but we'll put in some slightly different values. Now let's assume that we could see some sort of growth but really couldn't tell exactly what the numbers should be. So we can guess that the slope is probably negative something. OK and I'll intercept if pulsates have something. So what do we go with something like a negative 0.5 or negative point five Cape and that we can go with a pulse 2.5 and we'll see how accurate these numbers actually work out to be. So this is a stance right now actually wouldn't give too bad of a representation but it's clearly not exactly what we want. So we'll basically have to run these values through it see how they differ from our previous values and then decide exactly how much we want to change or train our data. Now keep in mind if our initial guesses are way off them only to train the data a little more it's going to take a bit longer to get an accurate results if our guest is very close to the real onset then probably won't require that much training and probably won't take very long to obtain an accurate model. But for now we'll just choose these valleys and assume nothing else. So let's create some x and y nodes. These are just going to be some placeholders. So I think literally just call them x and y. So this is just going to be chiefdom placeholder and we're just going to try to data type off against Sloat does it too. I'll copy this and I'll do the same. Y. All right. And you know what we might as well end to these values so we can do like a Y train and an X train. So I'm just going to copy these and just put them in the box. So this is going to be why train and train as these are probably going to be some of the values that will actually be used to train our model. But remember we're not going to be doing any of the training yet. We just want to build up the basics or the basis of our computational Groff. Once that's done we'll kind of run things a little bit then we'll work on seeing how to optimize the values we want and then how to train the data to obtain those. Now right off the bat we know what our linear equation is going to be so we should probably create a variable to present that we can call something like a linear model as that's exactly what we're going to be using. This is just going to be our formula and we'll just set this equal to w times B plus X or W times x plus B is actually what we wanted. If we wanted to be really clear we could put the brackets here but it's unnecessary as the order of operations implies that that will occur. So once we run that linear model it's basically going to take in our estimated value. It's going to multiply it by some inputs which will have to and so when we go to run it because this is a placeholder again and placeholders needs some kind of input when we go to actually run and evaluate those nodes and then we're also going to use our estimate for B. And it should give us some values back. We don't know how accurate or inaccurate they could be. So at the least we can just run it and see how bad or good Our guest is. So when do we actually do that now will create a new session. And this is just going to be T.F. session story again in that session variables will have to create an initializer for our variables remember this is a necessary step. This is just going to be T.F. don't global variables initializes should be this value here. And then we're going to run our session first on the initializers succession to run in it and then we're going to call the session that doesn't run now. I guess we'll run our linear model and we'll have to pass in some x values x values for this placeholder here. We can simply pass the now ex train and we want to compare the values that we get printed out to the values we see here. So if you remember from our place all the sexual We do the X equals and then in this case we could just enter an X train. Now obviously we want to actually view the results so I'm just going to print the results off this session. And I think we're just about ready to run this so we'll control it all . We'll run it or we can click on the run bus and up here. So let's examine the results. We got a zero, a negative point, five in a negative one and a negative 1.5. So let's compare those to our White values here and we'll see that we're actually not so far off these are pretty good guesses which you know should be what we would expect a next 0.5 is not so far off a negative one point 5 is not so far off a 1 but we're clearly not quite that we can be a lot more accurate with this model. Now take a look at how these values that we actually obtained differ from the values that we expected. So at this point in time these are the values we enter. And these are the values we expect as output. So the loss here is considered to be basically the differences between these values and these ones. So hopefully you can try to understand now when I say our model is designed to minimize loss by adjusting these values. So by adjusting the slope which is going to be this and our appliance septs which is going to be this our goal is to bring these values our output closer to these values. Now like I said the differences as they stand right now are considered the loss. So it will basically sum the total loss. We'll get some Saigo which will store loss in that variable and then we'll use some of the built intensive flow training functions, probably a gradient descent or something along those lines to help to minimize that loss by changing up the values here. Little by little. But that's going to be mostly safe for the next section. For now let's just create that last variable and examine how bad our model is as it stands right now. So what we want to do is just blow our linear model and we go above these training points if we want to create a last variable going to literally call it loss. And we want to basically get the differences between the results of our linear model and why train or in our case. Instead of answering in DS why training values Hayah we can actually just set our white placeholder and then pass them in when we go to run. So when we get the differences here and I'm just going to quickly bring in a comment which represents the values we obtain. So we had a zero. We had a negative point five and a negative one. And I think a negative 1.5. Let me just double check. Yes we did. OK so these are a comparison of the values that we actually received and the values that we should have received. So the way we obtain the loss is by subtracting either this from this or this from this and then squaring the results and then summing the results so that's how we obtain the total loss or the total amount of error. And again we're trying to minimize not just the loss between say this and this one and this and this one but total loss. So that means some of these points may be actually growing further apart and some of them may be growing close to it just as long as the overall loss is minimized. So the way we would do this is by saying T.F. dots we want to get the reduce some Okay and then we're going to get the ps. off basically after all squares. And we want to pass in the squares off our linear model minus Alwa Why so whatever values that we enter into this white placeholder. So this is essentially taking the difference between all of these. It's squaring each one of them so we get an absolute or positive value and it's just going to suck them all together to produce some kind of lost value. So now if we wanted to run our loss function so I can actually copy this and instead of running our linear model we'll now run our loss will need to have an extra value for our Y placeholder here because we are including this Y in our last variable. Okay. So we'll pass the Palsson X train and we'll pass the Palsson Y. We'll give it the Y train and see what kind of value we can obtain from this if we give this a run here that we get 3.5 as our total loss. Now that's actually not that bad and that's because we actually started out with some pretty reasonable values. Now look how things would change if we had something completely wrong. So if we had let's say a positive slope add a negative intercept. If we were going to run this then we would get something crazy like this loss soci 1.5. So this is really why it's so important to make a fairly good CAS right off the bat. As you can save your model a lot of training time by doing so. So I'll just stick with these. And like I said it's clear to us that this should be a next one and a one but we want our model to figure out that we don't want to just be telling them what to do all the time. Also not really machine learning. So with that done our basic computation of the graph is actually complete. We need to try to train our dataset and try to minimize this loss of value. So that's what we're going to be focusing on in the next section is building a clever way to train our model to best basically test a bunch of values that will eventually lead to a minimal loss value. So essentially the model is just going to have to specify first of all how many times we want our model to be trained. That's called the number of Polk's as well as the learning rate which is basically how by how much it's going to change these values here and then we can use some of the built intensive flow core functions to basically do all of that work for us and try to minimize the lost value again by adjusting these.

```python
import tensorflow as tf

# y = Wx + b
# x = [1, 2, 3, 4]
# y = [0, -1, -2, -3]

W = tf.Variable([-.5], dtype=tf.float32)
b = tf.Variable([.5], dtype=tf.float32)

x = tf.placeholder(dtype=tf.float32)
y = tf.placeholder(dtype=tf.float32)

linear_model = W * x + b

loss = tf.reduce_sum(tf.square(linear_model - y))

x_train = [1, 2, 3, 4]
#          [0, -.5, -1, -1.5]
y_train = [0, -1, -2, -3]

session = tf.Session()
init = tf.global_variables_initializer()
session.run(init)
#print(session.run(linear_model, {x: x_train}))
print(session.run(loss, {x: x_train, y: y_train}))
```

```
ear Regression Model
/Library/Frameworks/Python.framework/Versions/3.6/bin/python3.6 "/Users/ow
2017-09-22 15:03:30.533332: W tensorflow/core/platform/cpu_feature_guard.c
2017-09-22 15:03:30.533351: W tensorflow/core/platform/cpu_feature_guard.c
2017-09-22 15:03:30.533355: W tensorflow/core/platform/cpu_feature_guard.c
2017-09-22 15:03:30.533360: W tensorflow/core/platform/cpu_feature_guard.c
31.5

Process finished with exit code 0
```

So that being said, take a quick break, maybe review this stuff to make sure you're really comfortable and understand every single line of code and exactly what's going on before moving to the next part. Again some of this stuff can be really confusing if you fall behind in the early stages so if you are confused about some parts go back and watch them again or watch the tutorials on the individual nodes themselves. Otherwise we'll move to actually training our data in the section coming right up. Play guys previously we just worked on building on what computational Groff. So with the graph pretty much complete we can now work on training our data and optimizing our values of W and B and minimizing the lost value. Now with the last values 3.5 right now our model really isn't that bad. But we want this to be as close to zero as possible and we know we can guess at that. So what we will really need to do is essentially train our model to minimize this loss. We'll run a bunch of times that it's going to basically adjust the values that feed into law so it's going to adjust W and B because these are all variables and then by the time it finishes running hopefully it will have appropriate values for W and B that will minimize the loss as close to zero as possible. This will have to be probably pretty close to a negative one and this will be very close to positive 1 and then we can feed an anti x value we want and get the appropriate y value. Now although we are gradually going to be training the data itself we're just going to be using a bunch of tens of Flo's built in core functions to do so. So it's not like we have to go really complex into the behind the scenes like matrix algebra or any of that. We're just going to use tens of flows built in gradient descent function as well as its optimized functions. So it will start off just by creating what's called an optimizer. And I'll just store this in a variable called optimizer. We're going to basically set this equal to its dots. Train dots. And we want the gradient descent optimizer that's going to be this guy here. Now if we open up the brackets we need to put what's called the learning rate. So this is basically how much or by how much we're going to be modifying these values and this can be pretty tricky to get the perfect value as if we set this learning rate too low then is going to learn too slowly and we'll need to run it a lot more times to get an accurate result whereas if we set this learning rate too high then we're not going to get an accurate model because it's going to be adjusting these values too much. And so it's going to be hard to pinpoint the exact values we want. In this case they found a point 0 1 to be a pretty good learning rate. So essentially this will be just modifying these values by point 0 1 and we'll run it like a thousand times. So this should be an appropriate enough change. OK so with our will optimize Dunwell creates an actual training variable which will run the training itself. This will just be something like optimizer Daut we want to minimize the loss variable. Ok so this is going to use Alwa, our optimizer which will adjust the variables by point zero zero point point zero one and it's going to adjust them in such a way that will minimize our last function. Now our last function again is basically the difference between the current values of W and B and the expected values. So that this is the difference between the actual values of y and the expected values but these depend entirely on W and B. So those are the only two that are going to be adjusted. You remember X and Y are placeholders and W B W and B. All the variables so those are the ones that are going to change. So without Traina created it's just a matter of running our Traina a bunch of times until it has adjusted these values successfully. Now again choosing how many times our training runs which is called the number of ePOChs is again sometimes difficult to figure a pinpoint. If we run it for you many times and that's going to take a really really long time to train the data. Whereas if we don't run it enough times that it won't have had enough time to Ludd. This is why it's really important to find a fine balance between learning rates and your number of e Polk's but I've found about a thousand to do a good enough job. Again this isn't really a very difficult problem and as long as after we've trained it we get some précis close values to what we want. We know that the model has been trained successfully. So I'm just going to go down to the bosom here and I'm going to run a loop. I'll say something like for I in a range from basically zero to a thousand. So essentially we're running whatever we put in the loop a thousand times. Well in this case we're just going to have our session and we're just going to run it. And specifically we'll run our train variable which is going to try to minimize our loss. And we need to of course enter in some x and y values as we need y here we need X here. And these are placeholders. So we need to specify X to be actually you know we can just copy this because this is exactly what we'll be entering our training values for x and Weiss's copy and we can paste the N. Now after we finished running this and this will not get to print anything right now because there there's no call to print statement or anything. This will just have altered Alwa W and B. So why don't we print them out once this is finished running and see kind of where we're at with those values. So after this let's just correct the indentation there and we are just going to print a session to run and run just some values here. This will be specifically just our W and our will be. I just want to see what values these will take on towards the end if the data model has been trained properly W will be very close to a negative one and B will be very close to a positive one. So that being said we can give this a run through control or we'll run it let's see what values we get. You just open up the window here. So it looks like our first member of the array which is W's result is going to be very close to negative 1 so that's pretty much a negative one. We can say and this is pretty much a post of one to be. So it looks like our training has worked successfully and thanks to these functions here our optimizer and our gradient descent optimizer we were able to make the model basically adjust the values of WMP until we found something that was appropriate. So for these values being very close to negative 1 and pulsed have won our last will have taken on a very minimum minimal value and should be very close to zero. In fact why don't we print out just to see what exactly would have taken on. And I'm just going to do so with some formatted print statements so I'm just going to run our general session on W B and the loss. Okay. Now last I think we're going to need both y and x values so we'll pass an X train and y train as well. Let's copy these and I'll paste that. And at the very end we'll store some of these results in some variables specifically will say something like new w new B and new laws are going to be equal to the results. So then after this we can just format and print the results. So we go into print. We'll do something like a new W OK and then we'll have percent assets beside it we can put the actual value which is just going to be new to you. And we're just going to copy paste paste this time newbie this time new loss and then need to put in the appropriate variables here so new to all the UPN loss. OK so let's give this a run. Hopefully things will have worked out and I don't think I've made any errors. It looks like the stuff is all good here. So if we zoom in again, the new W is very close to the next of one newbie very close to the post of one and now a new lawsuit is very very close to zero. So essentially think about this as being this number we're at about 12 zeros in front of it now because we've successfully trained our models so we don't need to anymore in that regard. And running the model with some new data is really not going to take a very long time. I think it might as well just go ahead and run it with some new values. Now to see how accurate it is. So essentially because linear model is going to be the outputs if we run it then we want to inputs w once input x and B. So we'll simply run a linear model and will only need to pass in some x values I would W and B will have been already optimized as long as we've run it after this loop. So instead of printing out these values which we can then comment out you might as well you know I'll just comment on the print statements themselves. We are just going to run now. And you know we might as well print out right away we'll do Session don't run we'll run our Lenya model and we'll need some x values so we'll just say something like X equals we'll pass in an array of just some values here. Let's go with like 10 , 20 , 30 and 40. Let's see how accurate it is with those. So zoom out, give this a run, let's see, hopefully we'll get the appropriate values being printed. So that looks very accurate to me. We get about a negative 9 but negative 19 a negative 29 and a negative 39. And that's kind of what we would expect because we are essentially just doing one minus our x value.

```python
import tensorflow as tf

# y = Wx + b
# x = [1, 2, 3, 4]
# y = [0, -1, -2, -3]

W = tf.Variable([-.5], dtype=tf.float32)
b = tf.Variable([.5], dtype=tf.float32)

x = tf.placeholder(dtype=tf.float32)
y = tf.placeholder(dtype=tf.float32)

linear_model = W * x + b

loss = tf.reduce_sum(tf.square(linear_model - y))
optimizer = tf.train.GradientDescentOptimizer(0.01)
train = optimizer.minimize(loss)

x_train = [1, 2, 3, 4]
#          [0, -.5, -1, -1.5]
y_train = [0, -1, -2, -3]

session = tf.Session()
init = tf.global_variables_initializer()
session.run(init)
#print(session.run(linear_model, {x: x_train}))
#print(session.run(loss, {x: x_train, y: y_train}))

for i in range(1000):
    session.run(train, {x: x_train, y: y_train})

new_W, new_b, new_loss = session.run([W, b, loss], {x: x_train, y: y_train})
# print("New W: %s"%new_W)
# print("New b: %s"%new_b)
# print("New loss: %s"%new_loss)

print(session.run(linear_model, {x: [10,20,30,40]}))
```

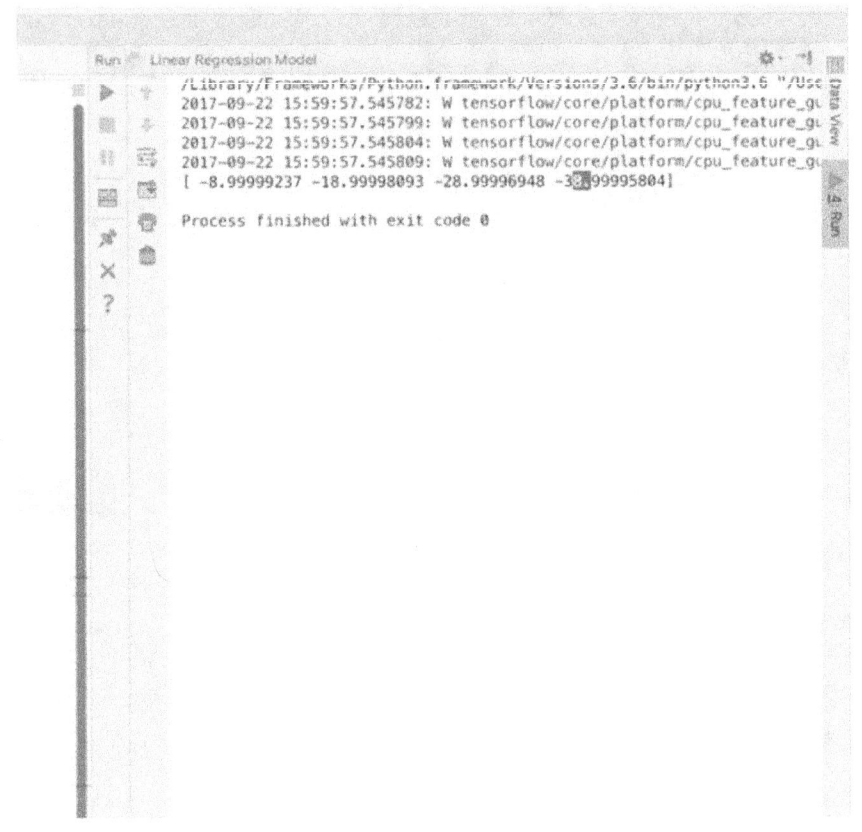

So with that being said I think we successfully trained our linear regression model and can finish up this section of the tutorial so it will explore pretty briefly some other ways of doing push much what we've done so it's just kind of new ways to arrange everything and to use tent's of flows built in estimator which provides us a bunch of high level stuff and can allow us to customize this process a little bit more. After that we have some other pretty simple programs to build which will help us to apply machine learning to a variety of projects. But otherwise you know at least the basics of getting a simple linear regression model Alper on the basics of how tense a flow might work in a machine learning project. OK so I hope this was easy enough for you guys to understand and it's clear enough now how to use it as tens flow is really fantastic. I mean just not having to take the axis like machine learning courses and stuff and how to learn about all that behind the scenes stuff is really fantastic because then you don't have to be particularly mathematically inclined or anything to be able to do this complex stuff you can just cool on the built intense flow library functions and allow them to do all the behind the work scenes. So I think what I meant to say was all the behind the scenes work. Anyway that's enough for me talking so check out our other tends to float you towards some really cool projects for you guys. Hope you understood this fine and liked it. And as always we appreciate the support. So hopefully see you guys in the next tutorials.

IMAGE RECOGNITION INTRODUCTION

What is up guys Nimish here with another tutorial on machine learning concepts using Python and Polychrome. So in this tutorial we'll actually be building up a model from scratch. And this is going to be a very simple image recognition tutorial. So we'll start just kind of by learning the basics of how to deal with images if I'm using Python. So we'll take a look at how to import images how to display them how to manipulate them and then convert them into the data format that we want then we're going to learn a bit more about our CFA or 10 image data set which essentially provides us a bunch of pre-trained images as well as the corresponding labels. So we're going to use the data from this massive data set to both create and train our model so that hopefully by the end it'll be accurate enough that it could predict with a certain degree of accuracy an image and what that image represents and then assign it to one of about 10 different labels. Now these 10 labels are not going to be chosen by me; these are just the 10 labels that our CIA F.A. or ten data set represents. So each of the images in that data is assigned to one of these 10 categories and we're just going to stick with that because it's slightly simpler than dealing with the CFA a hundred datasets. Now keep in mind as we build our model there's going to be a ton of different ways that we could go about doing it. I'm just going to show you one of those ways and it's up to you to explore some different methods. Maybe play around with the values and build up your own model towards the end and try to see if it's more accurate than the one we'll be building here. But otherwise let's go ahead and get started which is going to create and your project is how she starts it up here. And we want to find a safe place to save it.

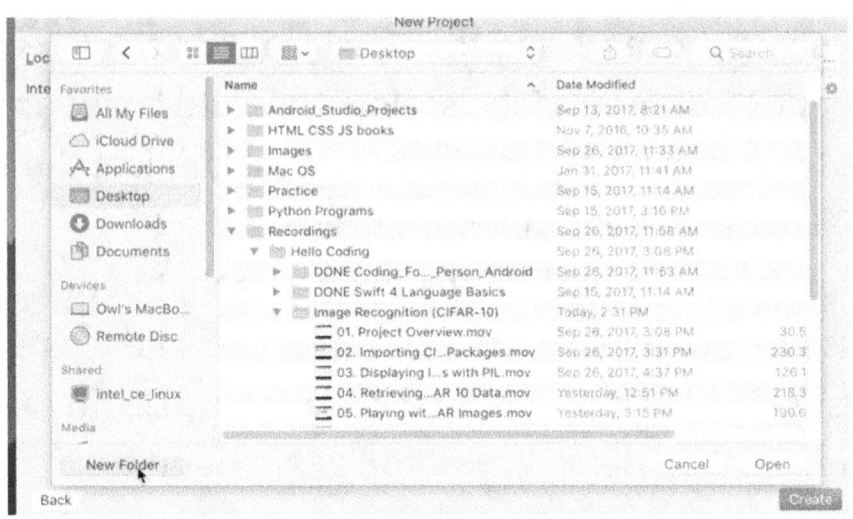

I could pick the desktop of something if I wanted but I should probably select a new folder. Let's just call this something like simple image recognition will click Create Cape's you can see fold. Open up and then we'll go to create this. Now I'm sure we do. Make sure you're using the latest version of Python 3.6 to say you have access to all the necessary frameworks. We will create our projects and there we have it. And when the project started. So like I said we're just going to begin by learning a bit more about the images themselves will take a few sections so that they will learn about the CISPA or ten days set how it's going to feed that data back to us and what we can do with that data that will take a look at how to build a powerful model how to build up the training data and manipulate it appropriately. And finally we'll work on testing or training our model. And then finally testing it to see how well it can predict the images we feed into it. So without further ado let's get started on the very first section. Just going to be a brief overview as to the projects of the products as a whole as well as the steps we're going to take to make it.

EXAMPLE CODE

Here's an example Python code using TensorFlow for basic image recognition:

Note: This is a simplified example to demonstrate the concept. Real-world image recognition tasks involve more complex models and training processes.

Python
from tensorflow.keras.preprocessing.image import load_img, img_to_array
from tensorflow.keras.models import load_model

```python
# Define the path to the image you want to classify
image_path = "path/to/your/image.jpg"  # Replace with your actual image path

# Load the pre-trained image classification model (MobileNet in this case)
model = load_model("mobilenet_v2.h5")  # Download the model beforehand

# Preprocess the image (resize and convert to array format)
target_size = (224, 224)  # Adjust based on model requirements
img = load_img(image_path, target_size=target_size)
img_array = img_to_array(img) / 255.0  # Normalize pixel values

# Expand the image dimension for the model (add a batch dimension)
img_array = img_array.reshape((1,) + img_array.shape)  # Add a new axis

# Make predictions using the model
predictions = model.predict(img_array)

# Decode the predictions (top result only for
```

simplicity)
top_class = predictions.argmax(axis=1)[0]
class_names = ["cat", "dog"] # Replace with your model's class labels

print(f"Predicted class: {class_names[top_class]}")
Use code with caution.
Explanation:

Import necessary libraries for image loading, preprocessing, and model loading.
Define the path to your image file.
Load a pre-trained image classification model (here, we use "mobilenet_v2.h5" as an example. You'll need to download this model separately).
Load the image using load_img and specify the target size for resizing.
Convert the image to a NumPy array using img_to_array and normalize pixel values (often required for image models).
Reshape the image array to add a batch dimension (required for most models) using reshape.
Use model.predict to get the predictions for the image.
Find the index of the class with the highest probability using argmax.

Define the class labels (adjust according to your model's classes).
Print the predicted class based on the index and class names.
Important Notes:

This example uses a pre-trained model. Training your own model is a complex process requiring a large dataset of labeled images.
Ensure the pre-trained model's class labels (class_names) match the actual categories it predicts.
This is a basic example. Real-world image recognition tasks involve more steps like data augmentation, validation, and potentially different model architectures.
Sources
github.com/Yoga-Final/Models

CIFAR 10 PROJECT OVERVIEW

Like ice. Now before we begin writing any code and actually building our project it's a good idea to take a moment to provide a brief overview of the project as a whole and talk about things like the steps we're going to take to make it as well as a list of topics we're going to be covering throughout. Now as I'm sure you gain from the intersection we can be building up a very simple image recognition model. Now this isn't as powerful as it could be but we just aimed at teaching you the basics and once you can build up the simple one you can work on a slightly more powerful model of your own. So by the end we want this model to be able to take in some kind of an image and then classify it into about one of ten different categories. So we'll start by installing the necessary dependencies. This is going to be basically installing and importing a bunch of libraries as well. We'll take a quick look into F.A. or 10 which is going to be basically the list of images that we're going to be using to train our model and provide those 10 categories I talked about earlier. Not once was I familiar with how to import and install the libraries we want.

```
Overview
1    - Build an image recognition model
2    - Install necessary dependencies (cifar-10)
3    - Go over how to display images
4    - Build training and testing data sets
5    - Build the training model
6    - Train and test the model
```

We're going to quickly go over how to display images using a couple of different methods in Python and we'll talk a little bit about how to manipulate those images as well as stuff like resizing, displaying different color scales and so on and so forth. Then we'll take a look at how to build up our training and our testing data sets from scratch. Next, once we have the data sets themselves, we can take a look at how to build up our training model and begin to train it. Now we'll be using a combination of our training data sets and the training data sets already provided by these libraries and frameworks that we imposed earlier. And finally we'll send a shot by testing our model and will do so by entering in some images and seeing which category is assigned to those images. So as I said earlier this is just going to be a really simple version. We're not aiming at making anything too complex just yet. Our goal here is to get used to Millia with the basics of not only tends to flow but all of the machine learning libraries that we can use and to get you used to the general process of how to do this. Now as I have mentioned several times it's always going to be a lot easier on you if you have the latest versions of pide charm and Python installed and both will come with the necessary libraries already downloaded and installed for us. We would need to import them into Polytone. That being said there will still be bits and pieces missing so that's what we're going to cover right now starting with gaining access to the CFA or ten libraries. So with that being said let's jump right in.

IMPORTANT CIFAR PACKAGES

Alright guys let's get started. We want to make sure that we have access to all of the data sets and the libraries that we're going to need to build up our project. Now I'm talking specifically about Iowa. Our CISPA is 10 data sets because when I began this project the first time I actually didn't have access to this library although I had almost everything else I didn't have the data sets and I had to download them from an external source. So first show you where to find the folder to check to see if you have it. And then also where to download the folder to gain access to the data sets as we're going to need them in this project. So to begin with we'll want to locate where we're going. We have saved our latest version of Python which should be 3.6 if you know where to navigate to it now. Otherwise I'll show you where it should be stored in my computer and likely your computer will be stored in a similar location. So if you just go to your main device Macintosh say HD and you just go to the library here or at least this is where it's stored in mind. Then I'm going to go down to the framework's good to go down to a

Python framework here. Next two versions and then a 3.6. Again it may be in a completely different location in your computer make sure that you've found this before proceeding any further. But once you found the correct Boesch and everything should be pretty similar from here on out. Next we're going to go to the lib tool library then down to 3.6. Then we're going to search for site packages which should be towards the bosom. This is the one that should be another folder. Next we are going to search for Cars us Trape this guy here not the data sets just Care us that we're going to search in here for data sets and there is data that selects it. You should see now there's a bunch of sea stuff. So the folder that I didn't have access to to begin with but we do need access to is going to be this one here this 10 dasht batches dash pie case or if we open this up you may or may not have this but if you open up then there's just going to be a bunch of data batch files batch all Massa read me and a test batch. So this is basically just access to a bunch of training and testing data. And this is just a massive image set essentially or kind of a few of them.

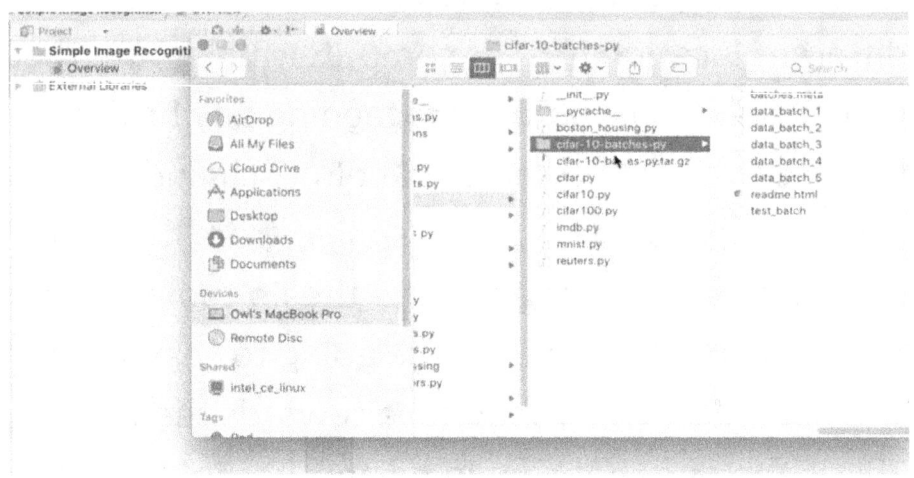

So it may be that you have this folder or not. If you don't have the folder checked see if you have the zip file if you have the zip file then go ahead and unzip it. And if you have neither of them I'll show you where to find both of these as you do need access to this folder to proceed any further. So assuming you don't have them I'm just going to open up a new instance of chromo of a browser you choose and just simply type in CISPA or 10. We're going to select the first link here. This gives us access to some download links for these two data sets. Now I'm not claiming to own any of this.

This was kindly provided by a few contributors but it was perfectly fine to use these datasets. Now as you can see CISPA R-Tenn. The set consists of a bunch of those two by those two color images in these basic 10 categories and these are the same 10 categories we're going to be using. As I said earlier we're going to keep this a simple model. If we wanted to make this complex we could go with CISPA or 100 which basically gives us X to 100 different categories but that also takes a lot more time to train. And so it can be a little less accurate if we're not willing to put in that time we're just going to keep things simple and stick with the 10 categories. So scroll down to where it says download him and we get to select the Python version. I already have it downloaded but you know what I'll download again anyway. So I was just going to take a second just to pause and add a. So now that this is finished downloading for me we want to open up our folder again and you can simply drop it from Chrome to find out we can open up to Windows finder and do the same thing. Just make sure it is in this folder in the data sets folder and you'll definitely want to unzip it as well if you did download the zip file. So with the unzips we're actually going to make a couple of modifications to these files here. I'm just going to select this one and open it with a charm so we're going to go to another one just like a charm from my list of applications. So that should open up CISPA or top pi. And we're also going to open up CFA or 10 dot PI again in Python so you can open with K. The average is going to select PI there. So try to make the default ID to open up your python files. And so we're just going to take a quick look at both of these files so forth. Starting CFA or dot pi is essentially going to make a call to our CFA or 10 dot PI file if we use the hundred then it would make a cool to that file instead. It really depends which one we are going to parse and when we call on our load batch file but we're not going to do that just yet. We'll save that for when we'll actually start to display and import some images. So I just wanted to open this up to show you guys exactly what it's going to do and it's essentially just going to load each of the data sets in a CFA or 10. In our case or 100 if you'd specified that one.

```python
# -*- coding: utf-8 -*-
import ...

def load_batch(fpath, label_key='labels'):
    """Internal utility for parsing CIFAR data.

    # Arguments
        fpath: path the file to parse.
        label_key: key for label data in the retrieve
            dictionary.

    # Returns
        A tuple `(data, labels)`.
    """
    f = open(fpath, 'rb')
    if sys.version_info < (3,):
        d = cPickle.load(f)
    else:
        d = cPickle.load(f, encoding='bytes')
        # decode utf8
        d_decoded = {}
        for k, v in d.items():
            d_decoded[k.decode('utf8')] = v
        d = d_decoded
    f.close()
    data = d['data']
    labels = d[label_key]

    data = data.reshape(data.shape[0], 3, 32, 32)
    return data, labels
```

So we can actually close this. We don't need to make any modifications to this guy here. We do have different needs to change just a couple of the lines in CISPA or 10 dot pi. So namely this once the directory name right now is called this one CFA or 10 Patches pie. But what this is doing is essentially linking to the same directory as the project has. And now unless for whatever reason you're saving a project in that site packages folder that's not going to be exactly what we want so what I would do if I were you is go back to this location where you saved this folder which is going to right click here. Cool on get info and see where it says where we're just going to copy this directory path name. So just come on. Copy. And I'm just going to replace it in here so yes you can see I've already done it but I'll just type it out again just for you guys with benefits so I'm going to set the directory name equal to in the quotes and then going to add this. And then of course at the very end you want to set your slash CISPA or 10 patches dot or dash pi. So just put the front slash there and then paste it in. And these two lines should be completely identical for me but just make sure that it has your whole path name in it so that when it goes to access the data sets Talma it's going to know exactly where to search.

```python
def load_data():
    """Loads CIFAR10 dataset.

    # Returns
        Tuple of Numpy arrays: `(x_train, y_train), (x_test, y_test)`.
    """
    dirname = 'cifar-10-batches-py'
    ######### line added for the image recognition stuff
    dirname = '/Library/Frameworks/Python.framework/Versions/3.6/lib/python3.6/site-packages/keras/datasets/cifar-10-batche
    dirname = '/Library/Frameworks/Python.framework/Versions/3.6/lib/python3.6/site-packages/keras/datasets/cifar-10-batche
    #########
    origin = 'http://www.cs.toronto.edu/~kriz/cifar-10-python.tar.gz'
    path = get_file(dirname, origin=origin, untar=True)

    num_train_samples = 50000

    x_train = np.zeros((num_train_samples, 3, 32, 32), dtype='uint8')
    y_train = np.zeros((num_train_samples,), dtype='uint8')

    for i in range(1, 6):
        fpath = os.path.join(path, 'data_batch_' + str(i))
        data, labels = load_batch(fpath)
        x_train[(i - 1) * 10000: i * 10000, :, :, :] = data
        y_train[(i - 1) * 10000: i * 10000] = labels

    fpath = os.path.join(path, 'test_batch')
    x_test, y_test = load_batch(fpath)

    y_train = np.reshape(y_train, (len(y_train), 1))
    y_test = np.reshape(y_test, (len(y_test), 1))

    if K.image_data_format() == 'channels_last':
        x_train = x_train.transpose(0, 2, 3, 1)
        x_test = x_test.transpose(0, 2, 3, 1)

    return (x_train, y_train), (x_test, y_test)
```

Now like I said this may or may not have already been done for you. I'm not sure exactly what kind of packages you've downloaded. It depends on which version Python and PIJ are using but I'm just going over the steps to take to make sure things are working correctly so with directory name or name correctly reassigned here we can now get this saved. I'm going to delete that extra line. So they give this a save and this should be good to go. We can exit out of that. So hopefully this should get rid of any errors that might have occurred otherwise. I know when I didn't have that package automatically installed then every time I tried to access those batch files it would say it couldn't find them because obviously they weren't quite there. So with that being said we're actually good to go and will save this and we're going to start a new file so we can begin building up our training model. So this is just going to be a python file just right clicks and says new file and we're going to call it something like image recognition. Traina OK and note the use of the underscore is probably a best idea especially for when you're passing and stuff like pathnames. So make sure this is a python file. We're going to click And now it gets Agos of course just going to start a blank file. So with that being said and having access to our CISPA or 10 libraries we are actually good to go. And all of the other packages should be automatically available to us. We just simply have to right click and press and store all imports or do what we need to do and we'll do those as we need access to them. So we can now move on to learning how to kind of modify and display our images and we're going to be using a couple of different methods using both the image library and imports from pill or Python image library. And we'll also take a look at how to do it using our NUMP pie and using nonplus and stuff like that for.

DISPLAY IMAGES PYTHON IMAGING LIBRARY

Pay everyone having downloaded CFA or 10 and now that we have access to about 50 to 60 thousand images for training and testing let's start to learn how to import images into our project display them and then manipulate them as well as what kind of manipulations will need to be able to feed these images into our training models. I think a good place to start with this would be at the very beginning with the easiest stuff and that's just going to be simply using P L or a python imaging library to import images. Open them up and display them once we are comfortable with that we can move on to the CISPA or 10 images of how to work with those. And then finally we'll finish up with the PI plot using pi plot to display our images in a slightly different format and that's going to give us access to a lot of extra functionality. So to begin with we want a basic import statement that's going to give us access to the Python imaging libraries image functions. So we're just going to say from p i l caps imports Howa image. Now this is giving you a red squiggly line. Probably because you haven't installed or imported P L so simply click on this hold Olt an option and return enter. And one of the options here should be to install P L and to import into the project. Now if you are using the latest version of Python Chaum this should definitely be available to you if you are using some of the older versions that might not be available and you'll have to go to the Python interpreter and download the package that way. And the same actually goes for a lot of these imports that we're going to be using if for whatever reason the install option is not there. Then we're just going to go to our whois preferences. We're going to go to either plug-ins and you can search for it here or you can search for your project. Go to our project interpreter, click on the ad Busson and then search for the package that you want. For example Kara ass can search.

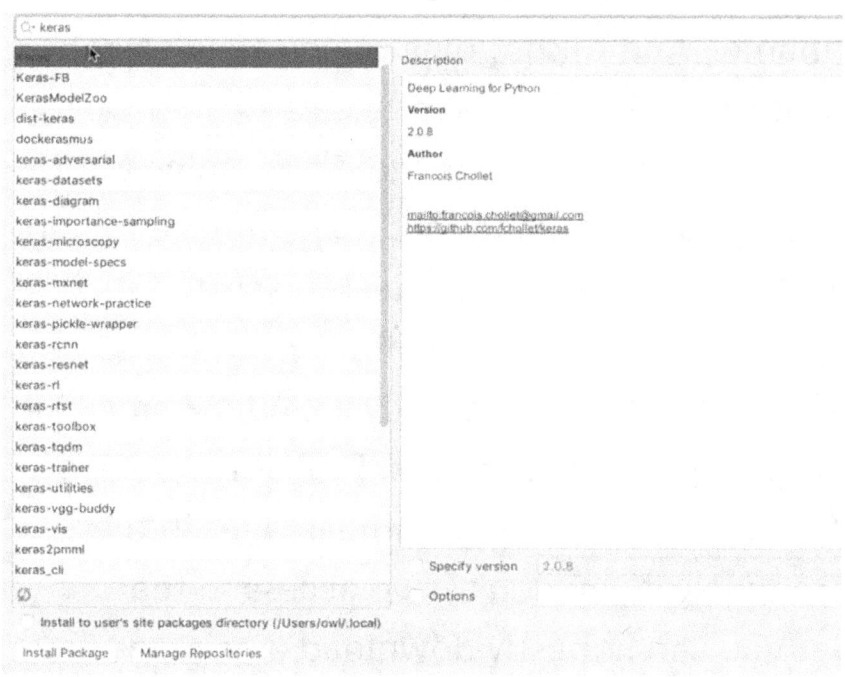

These already have the Karris package installed but any other packages you might want you can just install them this way as well. That being said, you can assume that you have access to the Python imaging library. So the way we would load images in the most basic form would be to simply Palsson a file or pass name as a string and create an image from that and then open it up. So step number one is to find a pause name and I'm just going to call this. I know it's going to be a cat image so I'm just going to call this cat's image pathname. And this is going to be called some string going to have to of course retrieve the actual part name of the image. So zooming out I was going to go to Finder and to my image folder which I know stored on my desktop sort of its image will probably be in a different route. So you guys now should have actually included some kind of a folder with some images. Probably not all of these but there should be some images in there. Alternatively if you don't have access to that folder you can honestly download any image you want off the internet provided you're not going to use it for commercial purposes or anything and just save it somewhere on your computer, find it and post in the past name in this case. I mean is this cat image for those cat lovers out there. This is what it should look like. Yes it is intentionally blurry and tiny It says only 32 by 32 so when it displays it should also be blurry and tiny. I'll explain why it was so small. A little later on once we start talking about the actual manipulation. Now just once you get the info command I will open up the phone. Once you get where it's located. So I'm just going to call this Back to the project posts here. And I'm going to have to add the name of the image so the front slash and then in this case is just cat dog Jay. So I have my path name should just be the string here to make sure it is spelled exactly and has the image name attached to it. We're going to call on the image to open and store this on a name cat's image and it's just going to be Image dots open. And we're going to pass in our cast image path name so lovely we can use the Palsson string directly.

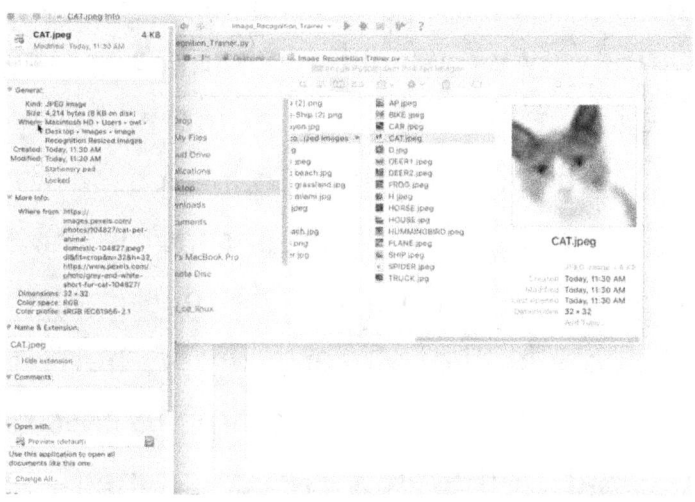

It's just kind of like this way best. It's easy to read. So now that we've opened the image or created it we're going to display it so we can say cat image dots show. And this is basically going to open up the loaded image thanks to this line in a new Windows so just zooming out. If I go to run this now we're going to run up here the first time you run it. You do need to do this. You agree an hour might not be available. So just click on that. And as you can see it's now open up this new window once it's finished running and my cat image is displayed directly to Alternatively and in my opinion a best way of doing this would be to have the user enter in a pathname. Once the program runs rather than relying on a hard coded string like this. So the way we would do that is by taking and using the inputs we take in user input simply by calling on an input function. So I can call this something like display image pathname. And this is just going to be inputs and we're going to enchant some kind of a user prompts here. This should be something like enter image pass name OK and we go and then we're just going to say display images self's is going to be Image door open and we're going to enter into a much pathname and then same thing as above we're just going to say display image to our show. So this is essentially accomplishing the same task as above it's just rather than relying on some hard coded string. We're going to probably use that to enter a pass named at run time and that's what input does. It displays this message and then whatever input the user enters at the end of it it stores that in this display image pathname. So what it could do is again just run this and now this time instead of all.

```python
from PIL import Image

# cat_image_pathname = '/Users/owl/Desktop/Images/Image Recognition Resized Images/CAT.jpeg'
# cat_image = Image.open(cat_image_pathname)
# cat_image.show()

display_image_pathname = input('Enter image pathname: ')
display_image = Image.open(display_image_pathname)
display_image.show()
```

Well I mean it's still going to display the Kattan image stuff because this is still up and running fact I'm just going to comment that out now note how it's actually prompting me to enter an image path name and it hasn't stopped running yet. So I'm just going to use that same path name as before. So copy this and I'll paste it right underneath. It should come out in green. Press enter and now it's going to do the same thing as above. This time displaying this image here just so happens that it ends in the same cat image path pathname. So that same image is going to be displayed up there. So this was the simplest form on how to display images just using the python imaging library and image from that clever. Like I said we're not going to be using this to manipulate our images. We're going to be using our pipelines. Sure we do that however. Let's gain a little bit more familiarity with all 10. So this section coming up is just going to be dealing with that a little bit. We'll show you how to load in images from that. Take a look at some of the images available as well as talk about the labels that are assigned to those images already.

RETRIEVING CIFAR 10 DATA

Like it is so far we've learned how to render and display an image by using some built in P L or Python imaging library functions and by passing in a path name which is kind of like a link to where that image is saved in our computer. However very often we'll be asked to render and display an image based on the image data itself rather than a location to where the image is saved. Now in order to do what we did in the previous section using the image data itself rather than this link We're going to have to use some Asawa pipe Plot functions but I'm not going to talk about those in this section. I'll save the discussion on that topic for the next section. For now let's just get used to this way of representing an image which is essentially an array of numerical values where each of the numbers in that array represents some kind of a pixel value. And let's get familiar with our say F.A. or 10 data sets as each of the images we retrieved from that data set will come back in this form. So it's a start. Let's switch over to our Web page where we downloaded our data here. And if he can't find this again just googled CISPA or 10 and it should take you here this should be the first link. So seriously all 10 is just essentially a massive data set off a bunch of these 32 by 32 pixel color images. Specifically there's 50000 training images and 10000 test images for a total of 60000 images.

< Back to Alex Krizhevsky's home page

The CIFAR-10 and CIFAR-100 are labeled subsets of the 80 million tiny images dataset. They were collected by Alex Krizhevsky, Vinod Nair, and Geoffrey Hinton.

The CIFAR-10 dataset

The CIFAR-10 dataset consists of 60000 32x32 colour images in 10 classes, with 6000 images per class. There are 50000 training images and 10000 test images.

The dataset is divided into five training batches and one test batch, each with 10000 images. The test batch contains exactly 1000 randomly-selected images from each class. The training batches contain the remaining images in random order, but some training batches may contain more images from one class than another. Between them, the training batches contain exactly 5000 images from each class.

Here are the classes in the dataset, as well as 10 random images from each:

airplane
automobile
bird
cat
deer
dog
frog
horse
ship
truck

The classes are completely mutually exclusive. There is no overlap between automobiles and trucks. "Automobile" includes sedans, SUVs, things of that sort. "Truck" includes only big trucks. Neither includes pickup trucks.

Now for each of the training and the testing images there is a corresponding value as an indexing kind of value. And each of the indexing values points to one of these indexes here in some kind of a label array. So for example let's say this is the very first image in my training data arbitrarily. So this is index 0 in my list of training images with a label corresponding to this image should also be 0. The reason being that zero points to this airplane label and indeed we are dealing with an airplane image. Now this pretty much applies to all of these airplane pictures just like if we were dealing with an automobile image the label that comes back might have an index of one which means it's an automobile. Automobile is index one in this kind of array of labels. So this might be a little bit easier to understand once we start writing the actual code for it. For now I just want us to imagine what kind of values we're going to get back. So if we were just retrieving the training values we'll basically get back to 50000 arrays that represent our images as well as 50000 labels one for each of those images that points to an index in this label array and the exact same thing goes with test images and the test labels is just that we'll have ten thousand off them instead of this massive 50000. So let's just explore how to gain access to these images and these labels. And then in the next section we can take a look at Pl Pipelet . Take a look at how to render and display our images and the labels. And then we can actually use the two together to load some Fouchier five or ten images. Now the first thing we might want is an array that represents all of these 10 labels here. And keep in mind that each of these 60000 images will fall into one of these 10 categories. So I'm just going to switch back to. We're just going to create a quick array that will represent that. And I'm going to call those labels just going to be an array or strings and let's say so the first string is airplane and you can speed this up if you want. I'm just going to basically copy an array of these guys. So awesome Abele And Bud then we have cats. Next up is the deer , which should be a string cape. After that we have a dog and should be a string. And then we have I believe frogs. Next up is going to be a horse with shovels telling that apparently and then we'll have a ship and finally we'll have a truck. OK so this is just an array of 10 strings for these 10 categories here. So now that we have this array of labels when we get back our labels from either our training or testing data we're just going to get an index into what this array will be and then we can just go into the survey, find the appropriate string at that specific index and then print that out again. For example let's say I get back some kind of an image of an airplane. Well it's labeled should come back as a number 0 which represents a 0 in this array. So that should point to the airplane label which is exactly what we want. So now the next step will be obviously gaining access to that CFA or data and to do so we're going to need an import. OK so we're going to say from ass dot datasets and be careful not to pick the carrots. I think underscore datasets is an option we want Karris dots data sets. Kate we're going to import and actually should probably zoom in so you guys can see this a little Besa going to import CFA or 10. Not the second one. All the CFA 100 we want are 10. And this is essentially going to be that file that we actually looked a little bit earlier when we were adding Iowa CFA our dataset to our computer so when we downloaded it and moved it into that site packages folder. So we have access to this file. We now have access to all of the functions inside of it, specifically one that is going to be used to load our data itself. So we're going to call on that function and then store the results in a tuple that may just show you which function it's going to be. We're going to use I will see them all 10 dot load data so not load Bachche we're going to call load data which will itself call on load batch. Okay. Now as I said and the results are going to come back as two tuples each of the tuples contains the image arrays and the labels that correspond with them and then the two tuples themselves are going to be for our training and for our testing. So let's just create a couple of tuples here. We're going to set them equal to these and within these two pools we need an image variable and a labels variable. Now typically for some reason a standard naming convention is to have the images themselves called something like X train. And the labels as y train. And I'm not sure why the capsule X and the lower case Y here. That's just a pretty standard naming convention so no sense in breaking tradition. And then we're gonna have an X test. Cape and a Y test. So these are essentially going to be arrays, probably arrays of arrays and this will contain our 50000 training images, the 50000 training labels and the 10000 test images and 10000 test labels there. Now as I said each of these are going to be arrays. So we would access a specific image by calling on X train or X test and providing some kind of an index. So for example. Let me just create some kind of an index variable that will literally call this index and to assess arbitrarily equal to 5. So if I wanted the six images in our X training data then I could go X train pass in the index 5 and just set the sequel to let's say display image so I'm actually going to comment this stuff out as we don't want to be calling on this again so I can say something like. Display image is equal to x train of five. Now this isn't going to be the image itself just like we had hayah. It's just going to be basically an array of numerical values. Now each of the values within this numerical array represent some kind of a pixel value which will determine how light or dark that pixel is. And as each of these images is a 32 by 32 image there are going to be essentially 32 times 32 pixels or numbers within this array. And so if we wanted the corresponding label for this image we could say something like. Display label is going to be equal to y on a school train. And we want to make sure not to mix up the training and testing here. And then again we would pass in the index and Shway it set 5 should just pass an index.

```
from PIL import Image

# cat_image_pathname = '/Users/owl/Desktop/Images/Image Recognition Resized Images/CAT.jpeg'
# cat_image = Image.open(cat_image_pathname)
# cat_image.show()

# display_image_pathname = input('Enter image pathname: ')
# display_image = Image.open(display_image_pathname)
# display_image.show()

labels = ['airplane', 'automobile', 'bird', 'cat', 'deer', 'dog', 'frog', 'horse', 'ship', 'truck']

from keras.datasets import import cifar10

(X_train, y_train), (X_test, y_test) = cifar10.load_data()

index = 5
display_image = X_train[index]
display_label = y_train[index][0]
```

And now oddly enough this will actually return an array with only one member in it. So we're just going to add the additional 0 to make sure that we're actually retrieving the number itself and not an array. So now that we have a way to access a specific image within our dataset and keep in mind this is again going to be in a gray it's not going to be an image quite like we've seen up here as well as the corresponding label. We can now work on how to actually render and then display the image.

So this stuff will become a little clearer as to why we're exactly why exactly we're doing what we're doing. Once it comes time to display the images themselves and to do so we're going to have to explore how to render and display images using Paey plot. OK so that's going to be this next topic coming right up. Phenolic just one shows you how to access our CFA all 10 datasets, how to load the data into some corresponding values as well as how that data is going to be represented. So let's get to actually rendering and displaying these images using pipeline's.

PLAYING WITH CIFAR IMAGES

Or Right now we know what kind of data we're going to be dealing with. Specifically the display image is going to come back as an array of families between 0 and 1 which will represent the pixel values in our images and the display label will come back as an index and we can use the index to display the appropriate labels from our labels array. So now why don't we actually use this information to render and display our image and then of course print out the corresponding label. Now I think the easiest way to do this is going to be to use Pylos. So I don't know. I guess it's not actually any easier to be honest than using our Python imaging library functions but will give us a lot more functionality and we could do a lot more with it. So we're going to of course have to import it as it is going to be yet another library. So we'll say from Matt lib case the map plot library we are going to import pipelines. And we're just going to call it T for short form now; rendering the image from this array is actually not so different from doing this kind of thing. We're actually going to call a different function than open and it's just going to be image show or show for sure. So we'll just go P L T taught him to show tape and then in the brackets we want to put the image up where or rather the array that we're trying to render in this case is just going to be a display image. And just like before we can store the results in some kind of a variable. So let's just say the final image or something equals the results. And then we'll just cool. Final image to show and that is going to show our results. Alternatively we could actually have completely got rid of this and just cool on TLT to show the OK PELTOLA show and this is going to do exactly the same thing. The difference is that using our pill library or the python imaging library were essentially opening the image and storing it in the variable then showing that whereas in this case we are converting this image array into the image itself and storing it within the PI plot. And then just showing the PI plot as a whole. So I'd rather do it this way just to show you the differences between the two. So why don't we go ahead and run this control. Oh we'll do that. And it's just going to take a few seconds to load up about 10 or 15 so I'm going to pause this and Stoss it once it's showing. All right so it took about 10 seconds or so. But as you can see this figure has popped up now a couple of things to note. One is that this picture is very blurry. And the fact is that this picture was shrunk down from I'm not sure how many pixels origine to a 32 by 32 pixel image hence why it's very pixelated if you squint your eyes you can actually see that this is a picture of a car. And the second thing to know is that this is showing in this figure it's not in that separate window like we had with the python image library. This is displayed a lot which is why we did P.L. t talk show here.

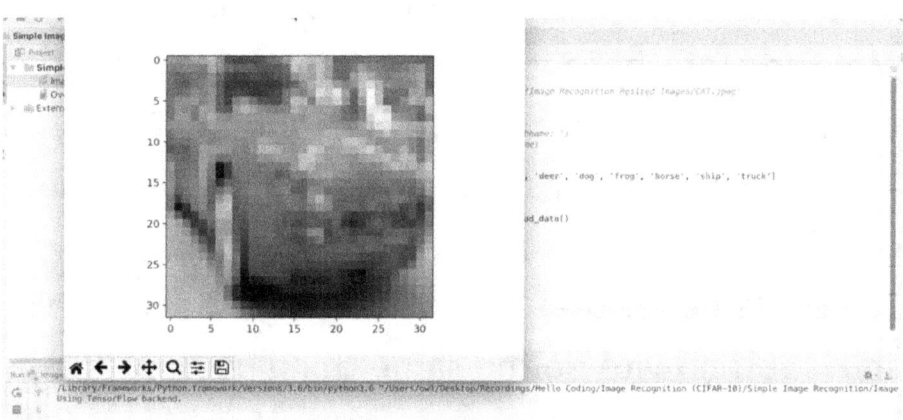

But for our sakes and purposes essentially accomplishing the same task show image show is just kind of rendering the image from our array anthem which is displaying the plot. OK so we are going to get the label printed out as soon as we close. And I totally forgot to print out our display labels so let me just do that. We're just going to cool print out labels using the index off display label which honestly should be named something different. But let's just give this another run through. OK so I'm just going to wait for that to load. But essentially we could do a pretty similar thing using our Python image library. So if I said we couldn't do it using that, that was a little bit of a lie. I just wanted to encourage us to use the PI plot functions because there's a lot more that we can do using pi plot than we can with our Python image library. So let's just quickly close up as you can see automobiles printed out. There is the correct label for that particular image. So before I show you how to do the same thing using an image library. Let's just go one step further and rather than importing the static rather than using a Nastasic image here, let's just import some input from the user. So we're going to say inputs we're going to prompt the user to enter an image index. And we're going to have to convert the results to an integer. Otherwise we're going to get some errors as you can't use string as an indexing variable. So we've seen how to do it using Piazzi. Let me just show you how to do it using our API.

So we're just going to actually just comment. So really quick and get out some code down here. We'll say something along the lines of the final image is going to be equal to image thoughts from Array. And then this way we compulsed and our display image which is that array of values and then we'll just call the final image doesn't show. And then we'll also print out the corresponding label this time we're going to take an input from the user. So let's give it another run. And again just going to take up a few seconds to load then we'll be able to add some index between 0 and forty nine thousand nine hundred ninety nine we'll get one of the images printed out as well as the appropriate label displayed. So let's just enter the index 10 k pressing and say here as you can see it is coming up with a label data really hard to see but that is in fact an image or idea. So a different window than with the PI plot. Now again although this is OK there's a few reasons I wanted to choose PI plots so first is that this image is tiny whereas if we are displaying on PI plot it kind of blows up a little bit. And secondly is that we'll get a lot of extra functionality using poly plot than we would with just displaying an image here. So I'm going to just comment this stuff out and on comment. Our original PI plot stuff. So as it stands right now regardless of whether we use this technique or whether we use this technique our image is coming back as basically three images superimposed on top of each other so one image contains red values. One contains green valleys and one contains blue valleys. So using someone'll Pipelet functions we can actually split the image and display just the red side, just a green light or just the blue side and this is just one of the things that we can do. So actually I'm gonna use a combination of the two that we just cut this and I'll put this down here. And that's just uncommenting this although we are going to make some changes so let's say we want to just display the red values from our image. So let's just call this red image and then we're going to split the red image into its three components so rather than just calling on the image name to show we are going to now say red green and blue all going to be equal to our red image don't split. And this is essentially going to spit out a red image although also to say this name till later it's going to split it into three color components. So now rather than just displaying a schmoozing image for our display image we can choose to display the red image. And then we're going to see map equals and then we'll just Palsson the string reds. Now if we go to show our plot here. So let's just zoom out and we'll give the Safari run. Then this is going to take whatever image we Palsson it's going to create just an image based on that data array. Then it's going to split it into these three respects of values that will use this to render just the read values for that. And then finally shove it. So let's go with that's also will be. Again let's go with index Phyfe will press enter.

```
# display_image_pathname = input('Enter image pathname: ')
# display_image = Image.open(display_image_pathname)
# display_image.show()

labels = ['airplane', 'automobile', 'bird', 'cat', 'deer', 'dog', 'frog', 'horse', 'ship', 'truck']

from keras.datasets import cifar10

(X_train, y_train), (X_test, y_test) = cifar10.load_data()

index = int(input('Enter an image index: '))
display_image = X_train[index]
display_label = y_train[index][0]

from matplotlib import pyplot as plt

red_image = Image.fromarray(display_image)
red, green, blue = red_image.split()

plt.imshow(red, cmap="Reds")
plt.show()

print(labels[display_label])
```

And as you can see it's taken that call image and it's only showing the red values. So we can do a very similar thing for just the green on the blue. But in those cases obviously it's going to show only those particular colors. All right so now you know how to play around with the images a little bit. So it is used in just a couple of different ways to display them. So I would encourage you to do is just kind of play around with these functions try showed the red values the blue values and just the green valleys of the image as well as just kind of go through these X train and X test data sets to kind of see what kinds of images we're going to be dealing with. And then once you're comfortable with that we can move to the next part. Well we'll be working on actually building up our model and the training data that we are going to be using. So whenever you feel ready. Head on over to the next section and let's start actually building up our image recognition model.

BUILDING A MODEL

Hi guys by this point we've learned a lot about how the data we're going to retrieve is going to come back to us essentially an array of values that represent the pixel values as well as what to do with that data. Once it comes back so in our case we were just retrieving some data from our CFA or 10 data set and we just output the correct image using a couple of different forms here. So at this point I think we know enough to start actually building up our image recognition model. Now before we get started on learning how to build it I'm just going to say that there are many different ways that we can build up image recognition models. Some will look very similar to what we'll be doing here. Some will look completely different and I'm not going to claim that even the one that we're going to be built to that building today is going to be the most optimal solution. It's actually quite tricky to add the layers which is what we're going to do in the correct order with the correct values in order to completely optimize our task. It's actually kind of an art balancing everything out to find the optimal image recognition model and the amount of Dacier seats and as well as the exact task of trying to accomplish is going to affect everything. Strom's it could. The way that we build up our model from the start as well as the values that we're actually going to enter in. So this is just going to be one of many many possible solutions. That being said, let's get into roughly how this model is going to work before we start building it. OK so we could use a basic sequential model and the way this is going to work is we're going to add the base model then we're going to add a bunch of layers on top of this model each of which will contribute something to the overall model and help with the accuracy or how it's going to perceive the data and is going to accomplish a bunch of different tasks. So as we go I'll try to explain exactly why I'm adding each layer as well as why I'm choosing the values that I do. But in order to really understand things you're going to have to play around with those values yourself and see how the model is going to change. But that being said, let's get started. We're going to, as I'm sure you've guessed, have to import a bunch of stuff into our project in order to be able to build up our model. So most of this is going to come from the cross library which provides a bunch of different functions and variables that will help us to construct our image recognition models so very often you'll see image recognition models starting with or being built from Cara's functions. So it will be safe from terrorists and we want cross-talk models to simply impose a sequential model which is basically going to provide us a way to oh I actually don't need those brackets. This will provide us a way to build a powerful model layer by layer. And that's going to be built in order hence sequential. Okay. So from this we'll need to add some layers in. So we go from Kara astore layers we'll import a few I will import a dense layer will improve probably a dropout layer. And I think we'll probably need a flacid as well. All right. So Also we'll have to put some more stuff from crosstalk layers and we want dots where we appear convolutional. Kate we want to import Conan today as well as a max Huling Tuti as well so we're going to be dealing with the arrays here now and will once be an optimizer. So it will go from Cara to stop optimizers. We're going to choose our Arwa SAGD optimizer. Okay. And then we'll also want some constraints or a constraint in our case we'll just use the one. So we're going to go from constraints and import Max looks completely Spolin, not wrong. Max Enorme so be sure not to pick the one with the underscore here which is what Maxson says in one word. Okay so that's a lot of imports but will give us access to all the pieces that we need to build up our model. And I'll try and explain why we need each piece again as well as why we use each particular value as we build the model up. Okay so we'll start at the very beginning just by declaring a model variable. We're going to set this equal to a new instance or see Quent shill. Okay, I finished it for me. Okay we'll just open up with a blank initialiser. Okay so we have the base model we want to start by adding layers to this so we'll simply call on model toward ad and then we can add whatever layers we want to this. So we'll start with the convolutional to the lab and this is just going to help us to specify stuff like the shape of the kernel we're going to use a bunch of constraints. And as you can see pretty much everything we could fill out but we're not going to fill all of this stuff out obviously as there are too many promises to deal with. So a good place to start is going to be with a kernel size now I could actually directly say kernel size equals or get just entered in 32 and it knows what I'm talking about. So those two I'm choosing because our image is all going to be 32 by 32. That's why we chose these numbers in our appeal Titos show. Okay. And that's again how all of the images of formis it anyway so no need to deviate there. All right. Next we want some convolutional steroids so we can actually just enter in some tuple here. In this case we'll pick three and three and this is just going to mean that's going to traverse our x direction as well as the y direction the same increment. And this kind of a way to specify how much of the data we're going to be dealing with at any given time so we can't take all those two by first pixels, we can just work with a three by three block at a time. Next up is going to be the input shape. OK this one I can actually say in put shape equals right. And this is just going to be a tuple of Thalys, what we know is going to be 32 by 32. So essentially 32 32 and they're going to be three images within that. So you remember when I talked about our images being red, green and blue. And that's why I spent the time talking about this. That's why we have three because we want all three images together. OK so next up we want to specify some kind of an activation and you know what it might be easier if I actually zoom out. And so this one we're going to use reglue. And this will be instead of soft marks. You can try out with either of them really just generally gives us the straight line whereas soft mix is a little more curved. I think we'll use the same padding so specify padding to be equal to the same. And it's the same or valid but we'll go over the same set of input images and output images that you know have the same padding. And then we once you specify a kernel constraint and we're going to set this equal to our Max. Max norm And we want to put some value in this case will choose just the values 3 because that's going to be a kind of our stride as well. So this very first layer is just kind of setting up the base for our model as sequential doesn't provide too much stuff. Next we'll want to just kind of downscale the model a little bit so we're going to add the max pooling to D. Okay. And we're just going to answer in a two by two to Paul. I guess I should specify that this is going to be the pooling or the pool size. Okay. So just close off the brackets. All right. Next up before we add our dense and drop out outlays will once you Classen our model so that we're dealing with just a single one dimensional array as our first two counterparts took into the arrays but dense and dropout will want to deal with only a 1 D array.

And I'll kind of go back once we finish building our model and explain these in a little bit greater depth. Just to kind of review everything so we're just going to add the flacid and they should be capsule F and just open and close the brackets. And now we can actually start adding our dense layers so we'll just let me move over Lisbet So we'll go a model to add and we're going to add one how it DENSELOW is now will actually add a couple of these but let's just start out by adding in the size we'll be dealing with which will be 5 12. This essentially is 32 by 32 and we want to divide this by two because we're dealing with just a two by two pool size. Next we'll specify the same activation and the same kernel constraint as before. So we can actually just copy these in and get rid of padding just do so. Copy that and we'll just paste in here and discover that padding we don't really need in the SO with one dense layer added. We can add in a dropout layer. And then finally our second dense layer on the model will be just about complete. So we can add in a dropout. And so the value of a 0.5 in him. And finally we're going to again finish up with that last dense layer.

This time we'll just enter in a turn and we'll use a soft Max activation I think. So Soft Max and that is just about it. So the last thing we need to do is compile this model before we can start training it. And then of course we need to add in our training data and we might as well do it now although I'm not going to train it just yet. We'll go modeled or compile. Now we want to add in a few things here. We want to add in some kind of law so we're going to go to loss equals and we'll go with a Kassa Oracle cross and Trape think it is spelled right. This is just specifying one of the ways we can define some kind of a last function. OK then we'll go with some kind of an optimizer and the optimizer we are going to be using is going to be SAGD. S g d. And we'll enter at some kind of a learning rate. So learning rate equals let's go with a point 0 1 that's kind of the recommended value. And at the end all we want is our accuracy metrics because we want to measure how accurate our model is going to be. So let's go with metrics and we just want accuracy. We should probably put this inside of an array as we could specify other metrics that we'd won in this case. I actually only want accuracy anyway. OK so we've written quite a lot of kind of confusing stuff if we've never built models before. So let's kind of go through layer by layer of our model and discuss what we're doing with each of these layers that we're adding and why we're doing it. So we typically start with a convolutional 2D model or we are going to want to put this right at the very beginning. And this helps to ensure that the orientation of the image isn't going to affect anything. It's not going to have a negative effect on the accuracy of our recognizer as well as specify several crucial pieces of information such as the input shape and the activation function we're going to be using. And a couple of other Sessa pieces of information here. This next layer on Max pooling to me is kind of there to make sure that our image isn't going to ignore any parts of our image so to buy to size and shows that it's going to cover pretty much every part of the image to give a slightly more accurate prediction. Next up the flacid is just as two sets up for dents and dropouts which want only one D-Rays as we kind of dealing with Tuti phrases these might imply that as of this point remember the data that we're retrieving from the images is going to be basically a 32 by 32 matrix. Next up and perhaps most importantly all our dense layers. So the dense layers of the head basically try to remember which characteristics make up each kind of category of images. So for example let's say we had a bunch of images of ships. Well, we might recognize their ships if they cycle a blue background based on the sea as well as the general shape of the image and just some distinguishing features. So we generally want a number that's fairly high that will give a higher degree of accuracy. But if it's too high it kind of goes into too great a detail and forgets what the overall image is trying to represent. So that's kind of why we use our dropout function next or our dropout layer. And this is also going to ensure that not only are we going into too much detail and ignoring the big picture but that the model doesn't become lazy in the US to try to forget new examples. S'il kind of helps it to pay attention to every new example and every new training piece of data that comes in. And finally the soft Max dense layer just for an extra degree of accuracy kind of approaches it using a couple different activation functions. And because we typically finish with some kind of a dense. Anyway And finally the compile line down here is just going to specify what kind of loss function we are going to be using what kind of optimizer and the learning rates as well as in this case we just want the accuracy metrics rather than any of the other pieces of information that could come back to us. All right so with that being said that is our model pretty much built from scratch. And that's actually all it really to

```
# cat_image.show()

# display_image_pathname = input('Enter image pathname: ')
# display_image = Image.open(display_image_pathname)
# display_image.show()

labels = ['airplane', 'automobile', 'bird', 'cat', 'deer', 'dog', 'frog', 'horse', 'ship', 'truck']

from keras.datasets import cifar10

(X_train, y_train), (X_test, y_test) = cifar10.load_data()

index = int(input('Enter an image index: '))
display_image = X_train[index]
display_label = y_train[index][0]

from matplotlib import pyplot as plt

red_image = Image.fromarray(display_image)
red, green, blue = red_image.split()

plt.imshow(red, cmap="Reds")
plt.show()

print(labels[display_label])

from keras.models import Sequential
from keras.layers import Dense, Dropout, Flatten
from keras.layers.convolutional import Conv2D, MaxPooling2D
from keras.optimizers import SGD
from keras.constraints import maxnorm

model = Sequential()
model.add(Conv2D(32, (3, 3), input_shape=(32, 32, 3), activation='relu', padding='same', kernel_constraint=maxnorm(3)))
model.add(MaxPooling2D(pool_size=(2, 2)))
model.add(Flatten())
model.add(Dense(512, activation='relu', kernel_constraint=maxnorm(3)))
model.add(Dropout(0.5))
model.add(Dense(10, activation='softmax'))

model.compile(loss='categorical_crossentropy', optimizer=SGD(lr=0.01), metrics=['accuracy'])
```

Unlike with tens of flow we didn't have to build up a neural network House self with a bunch of the different nodes we can actually just use these functions to do all of this for us. And again I want to rehash the point that this isn't the only way to build up our image recognition model nor is it necessarily the most optimal way. It's just a simple way. And at one of many possible ways that we could do this. So by the very end I would encourage you to do it once you're comfortable having built the Up-Hill model completely. It's not done yet. We saw quite a bit of work to do but towards the very end got to play around with these values a little bit. Maybe add some more layers and take out some of these layers that we've added. And again just kind of modify these values to see how your accuracy of your model changes. So for example if I increase this number in our first layer do I get a more accurate model. Or does it start to focus too much on the minute details and less on the overall big picture. But that being said the model is built on a model is built so we can start moving on to actually training this model. Now before we can train the model we need to build up some training data we shouldn't feed in the same data that we treat we should modify a little bit. So that's what we'll be doing in the next section that we can start training our model and finally finish up by testing it and its measure of accuracy. OK so I would encourage you to do a little bit more research into this and then we'll be right back.

BUILDING TRAINING DATA AND TRAINING MODEL

All right guys with a basic model built on all the layers that we want added. We're now almost ready to begin training our model. But before we can do so we want to build up a training data set. Now we don't want to use the same x and y training values that we were using with our ECAC IFJ or 10 dataset. We just want to modify these a little bit. So we're just going to create some training data just underneath our print labels here and above these import statements and then we can begin actually training our model. So I'm just going to start with a quick import so we're going to go from Cara astore you tills. We want to import and P utils and I'll show you where we're going to use this in just a second. Let's begin our basic set up. OK so this new X and Y training values. I'm going to set up a new X train and a new Y train. So we'll basically take all of the training values from our CFA all 10 data sets so we have the X train, Y train X test and Y test. We're going to basically take these and we're going to come out with floats divided by 255 and then we'll just pretty much use that. OK so I'm going to say the new X train is equal to our current X training. But we want to cost this as a type and we're going to go Sloat thirty two. Except that float those two need to be as a string here. I'm going to do the same for our X test. So a new X test except we're going to obviously take our X testing data and X training. Next up we want to convert or worldcat divide these by 255 so that we get values between 0 and 1. So we'll say the new X train. Equals our new X train. Divided by 255. Or we could just say divide equals 255 and we'll do the same for when you X test again. Divide equals 255 and I'll convert it into the values between 0 and 1 which is how we want to be feeding our values into the model. OK and lastly we need to convert our labels to a whole wide train and R Y test into a readable format case and this is why the N P tills are going to come in handy. So we'll basically say this is why the train is going to be equal to p you tildes dots too categorical. And we're going to just feed in our current y training values which we just called BY train. So give Street that in and then we'll just do the same for our Y test. So just going to copy this and paste it this time. This will be the reason for the test. And we're going to obviously take in our why test instead. So with our new training and testing days complete we can now begin actually spacing or testing our model. So we haven't run it to compile it yet but we will do this in just a little second here. I'm just going to zoom out so we can see the big picture. So the way we actually begin training or facing our data is simply to cool the model to fit. This is a built-in function and then we're going to pass in some parameters, namely because we are going to be training on a model we want to pass in our new X train. Okay. And then our new white train, not the test we want to train them, we want the number of times it is going to run or the number of parks. So we'll go Hawks. I think 10 should be good and that's actually the recommended value there. And lastly we'll want a batch size again it recommends Ducey to here so we'll stick with the recommended value of 32. All right. So we're almost ready to run. I just want to do one more thing because running this and trading it is actually going to take quite a lot of time and I'd rather not have to repeat myself and have to train this all over again. So I'm going to take whatever model we finally train and I'm going to save it to a file. Now the benefit of doing this is the fact that we'll be able to form a completely different file call upon our already trained model so that every time we run this program we don't have free training. If we don't take this last step then pretty much every time we want to recognize an image we'd have to run the model all over again and retrain it. Now in order to save our model I'm going to save it to an 85 mile type which means I'm going to have to import my 8 5 P Y. Again for us this imports very likely this won't already be installed so you might have to separately install the package if the option doesn't come up here and it's still giving you errors again just go to your preferences and find it in the project as interpreter. Just click on the plus and it'll take you to a place where you can find all the packages you need.

```
display_image = X_train[index]
display_label = y_train[index][0]

from matplotlib import pyplot as plt

red_image = Image.fromarray(display_image)
red, green, blue = red_image.split()

plt.imshow(red, cmap="Reds")
plt.show()

print(labels[display_label])

from keras.utils import np_utils
new_X_train = X_train.astype('float32')
new_X_test = X_test.astype('float32')
new_X_train /= 255
new_X_test /= 255
new_Y_train = np_utils.to_categorical(y_train)
new_Y_test = np_utils.to_categorical(y_test)

from keras.models import Sequential
from keras.layers import Dense, Dropout, Flatten
from keras.layers.convolutional import Conv2D, MaxPooling2D
from keras.optimizers import SGD
from keras.constraints import maxnorm

model = Sequential()
model.add(Conv2D(32, (3, 3), input_shape=(32, 32, 3), activation='relu', padding='same', kernel_constraint=maxnorm(3)))
model.add(MaxPooling2D(pool_size=(2, 2)))
model.add(Flatten())
model.add(Dense(512, activation='relu', kernel_constraint=maxnorm(3)))
model.add(Dropout(0.5))
model.add(Dense(10, activation='softmax'))

model.compile(loss='categorical_crossentropy', optimizer=SGD(lr=0.01), metrics=['accuracy'])
model.fit(new_X_train, new_Y_train, epochs=10, batch_size=32)

import h5py
```

And that goes not just for this package but to any of the previous imports that you might have been struggling with. And so this is finally going to give us the opportunity to save our model so we'll simply call on model will say it'll save and then begins postes in some file name. And I know there aren't any extra files other than this over a few text files but we're just going to ignore that and we're going to write in some new file names so that it will save the model and all of its data to this new file. We can call this however we want. I think something like trained model and to fly if we want the H5 extension is appropriate. So at this point in time we are just about ready to run this so we can get this a save. And one final run through or I guess this will actually be our first time I'm running the actual model. Now actually before we begin broth and said Mr. Parks let's just say it's a 1 so that if there are any issues throughout the running of this program will only run through the data once and we'll be able to pick up on those issues right away if we actually set this to 10 right off the bat that it's going to run through all 50000 images 10 times and that can take anywhere from half an hour to an hour to complete. If we just do the one Pawk this should only take somewhere between five and 10 minutes and so we'll be able to much more quickly pick out any errors that might exist in the code. Although this should be error free at this point. So I'm actually just going to get rid of this print statement now as well as these other show functions. So rather than deleting them I'm just going to comment them out as well as actually pretty much all of this stuff too. I think for now the search is safe to come on now especially because I don't want to use it to be entering an index as input so just as long as we have access to our data here we have the correct imports. Our labels. I think we are just about to go. So let's give this a run through. We'll run it to make sure you do have this image recognition Traina file selected. If you don't have that then go to your run window and click on this run and then select the file from that. So in a second if all goes well then we should pop up with this kind of interface that is going to begin training. So don't worry about those red warnings at the beginning. Those are just warnings. So we can completely ignore them. They're basically saying this can run faster if it was in a different program. So as you can see it's running through the data. There's 50000 pictures and labels to run through. This tells us which one we're currently on. This is just kind of like a progress bar tells us how much time we have left. The current loss and the accumulated here. So I'm just going to let this run through a bit of a pause. Actually I'll probably end the recording here. We'll run through at once if there are any issues at the end then we'll fix the issues and then move on to running it the full 10 times to properly train our model. Otherwise I'm going to just let it go if there are no errors at the end of this then we can basically start running it again just run it change a number of parks to see 10 instead of just one and then come on back for the final section where we will begin actually testing the model to see how good it is.

FRAUD DETECTION INTRODUCTION

What's up everyone? Never share with another mammoth in search of tutorials on machine learning models written in pite Chaum using Python. The model we will be building today is going to be a simple fraud detection model. Now this fraud detection applies specifically to credit card fraud detection. So our model will basically take in a list of transactions, some fraudulent, some legitimate and scones outputs. The percentage at which you can calculate fraudulent fuss is legitimate. How accurate it is and if a little bit modified will output whether or not a specific transaction is fraudulent you'll adjust. If we pass them in one by one. Now keep in mind as we go through this tutorial that there are many different ways to build up this particular model as there are with most machine learning models. I'm just going to show you one way in which we can construct it. And the way in which it shows we can build up a very similar model using completely different provinces and outputs either the same results or worse result or perhaps even a better result. And specifically with machine learning models there's always going to be room for improvement. There's always going to be ways in which we can improve the accuracy until we're at 100 percent which is pretty much unobtainable. But that being said, let's get started right away. We're just going to create a new page on projects. I have a pie chart open and as always I'm kind of expecting that you have the lace version of Python This is 20:17 put 2.3 and the latest version of Python installed this is going to be so much easier if you do as it will give you access to basically all of the packages that will need to install and impose. Also if you don't know anything about tens of flow we are going to be using a lot of tent's flow techniques. So be sure to watch our tutorial on the intro to tens of flow and how to build up a simple computational growth. Otherwise let's get started. We'll create new projects. The first thing we need to do is choose where we want to save this will just create a new folder on the desktop and it's always a good idea to do exactly that. Just start off by creating a brand new folder. Let's create You called it here. I'm going to call this credit card fraud detection click Create choose up folders you can see as crazy down and open create and to make sure that you are using the latest version of Python. Even if you have the latest version installed it might not necessarily be that version that we're using so be sure to do that. So the rough order in which we go and do things will be as follows. I will start off just giving a brief overview as to the project as a whole but basically will be first of all exploring the data set that we're going to be working with the subtlety of pre-compiled data. It's kind of difficult to get our hands on a bunch of fraudulent first legitimate credit card transactions and there's data that's already nicely compiled and converted into numerical format which we can feed into our model as well. It has a corresponding budget versus fraud outputs as well. Once we're comfortable with the data itself we'll work on manipulating it a bit and we'll do so in such a way that it will be easy to fit into our model and our model can understand and predict with accuracy. Next we'll work on building up our actual computational graphs with a series of nodes and functions of connect the nodes and help to run basically inputs through that series of knows this and many neural network will be building up and outputs either 1 or 0 depending on whether or not that credit card transaction is legitimate or fraudulent. And finally we'll end up with.

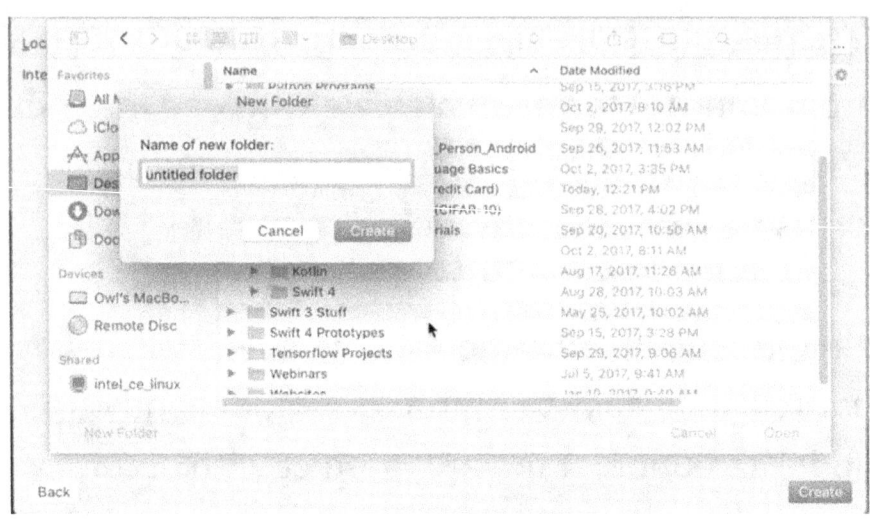

By creating a session , we'll be first trading our model by running a bunch of data through it and then testing it to see basically how well-trained our model is and how accurately it can predict a credit card transaction. So just one a quick second just to say thanks for all the support we really appreciate that you guys are interested in what we do and continue to support us and know that particularly these machine learning tutorials do cover some pretty confusing topics. So I've tried to make it as simple for you as I can and explain what's going on at each step. But if you find yourself lost then feel free to go back and watch this section again. And there are some topics which I don't manage to cover in great depth, so definitely go ahead and research stuff on your own time. It is important to understand what's going on at each step before you continue on to the next one. That's like I said it's easy to get lost and we're covering some pretty confusing stuff here. But otherwise I hope you guys enjoy this tutorial. I hope you learn a lot about machine learning and how to build up these models. Again this is just one of many ways we can do things. I'm just here to show you one way. But once you know how to do the basics of it then feel free to explore things on your own time so just different parameters in different numbers. So on and so forth and also be sure to check out some of our other machine learning models that will be building too. So without further ado let's get started with a brief overview where we'll go more in depth as to what we'll be doing in this project as a whole.

CREDIT CARD PROJECT OVERVIEW

Hi guys, I'm going to take a couple of minutes here to provide a brief overview of the project as a whole and kindly talk about the order in which we're going to implement our various tasks. So as I'm sure you know by now we're going to be building a basic credit card fraud detection model and the end result of this model is that we want to be able to enter a transaction with several of its features it to various numerical values and the model will output whether or not that particular transaction is fraudulent or legitimate. Now a big part about building our machine learning model is going to be obtaining some valuable training and testing data and we're going to be using this dataset found at this particular link. Now I will copy and paste this link into the python file at the very beginning once we start learning about it or feel free to just review this section and just type this particular link into your browser should take you right to the data set which you can then download. But I'll go over it with you guys on how to do that. Anyway this is how we're going to be saucing we'll just talk a little bit more about the data set how we're going to use that and what exactly all the values are passed into this data set mean once we have access to the set which will import into our project we'll work on manipulating this data into a format that we want to work with. This will be clipping off unnecessary values splicing things into X training and weight training as well as x testing them while testing policies as well. So once we are familiar with the data set and are happy with the format in which we end up with. We can start actually building up our model and what we can do so as a tendency of slow computation graphs might take a few sections depending on how complex things become.

```
- Credit card fraud detection model
- End result: Enter a transaction with several features and model will predi
- Start by learning about data set found at https://www.kaggle.com/dalpozz/c
- Manipulate data set into format we want to work with
- Build the model as a tensorflow computational graph
- Train and test the model
- Output accuracy when comparing predicted and actual values
```

So if you've gotten the basics of building up how tense of flow computational cross I do recommend that you watch our interesting Henslowe tutorial which I describe a lot of the different components and how they all come together. This will be at the end of the day a linear regression model. So it will be a little more complex than the one we build in the sense of flow intro. So off to the model is built all of the components of the graph have been put together we can work on actually training and testing Albemarle by creating a new session and then running the particular tensest that we built bypassing in some first training data to obviously train the model and then testing the model using some separate testing takes. And our final result would be to output the accuracy of our model itself. And this will be done by comparing the predicted values of what we think we should get versus what we actually get or the actual values. Now as always this is just one of many many different ways of building up this model so I'm not going to guarantee again that this is going to be the most efficient way. Well the most accurate way of doing things. I'm just here to show you a fairly simple way I think of doing things. And just one of the various ways in which we can build up this kind of a model as well as teach you about the various tensor components and just generally some machine learning techniques in Python and Python. So with that being said let's move to our first section feel free to open up a browser into a browser you choose and copy in this link here. And we'll be right back by learning about our dataset.

INTRODUCING A DATASET

We're going to take it to implement it. We should know that the first step is going to be to become a bit more familiar with the data set that we're going to be using to derive some training and testing data. So I just open up a new browser and copy and paste the link I provided in the overview. So just make sure you'll probably have to type it in manually but this is going to be the one that we're going to be using and we'll link to this big data set that provides a bunch of credit card transactions. Now normally I'd tell you to download it but I should have provided the data set to you guys anyway because otherwise you need to actually log in and create an account that says download the data set. So I'll try to include it in some kind of a Resources folder or something and make it obvious to you as to where it's stored. I'll show you how to import into the actual project that's going to be the easiest way to go towards the end of this section. So now let's just learn a bit more about what the data is and what all the values represent. So as you can see this is just under 280 five thousand credit card transactions with just under 500 of them being fraudulent and the rest being legitimate. Now this is already kind of a problem because as you can see only points 0 7 2 percent of the transactions are fraudulent which means the data is highly skewed and highly biased towards legitimate transactions. So if we were to use the data as it is this would cause our model to recognize legitimate transactions a lot more often than fraudulent ones would end up producing some pretty skewed results. This is where our data manipulation is going to come in handy because we'll find a way to hopefully kind of balance this out. And equilibria the fraudulent and the legitimate transaction where he sings. Otherwise like I said we'd end up with a very biased model. So out of all of these transactions each one of them is going to be transformed into these 28 different figures which are all going to be different numbers and these numbers just represent various features of the past each particular transaction. Now there is some kind of a PCA transformation function that is put in place to convert each of the features inside a numerical value. And unfortunately I can't provide more information about the nature of that function itself.

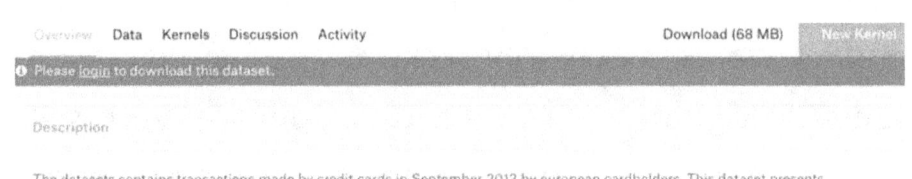

Which also means that if you are feeding data into the model then you need to use either the same or very similar function. That's why the end result of this function of this particular model we're going to be building is more on assessing the accuracy of the model then taking in just one or two transactions and outputting fraudulent or legitimate. But that being said there are some features of each transaction that are easy to understand the time and the amounts as well as a 1 or 0 that represent fraudulent or legitimate transactions respectively. So we'll get to know the data a little bit more. Once we start looking at some of the actual numbers involved, we can now start to think about what we're going to use for training and testing data and what we're going to use for our X train and white train and then X test and test respectively. So likely the X train and X test will contain some number of these transactions and will contain these features one 3:28 whereas the white train in the Y test which is going to be kind of the output fraudulent adjustment will be this either 1 or 0 value matrix. And then obviously we'll take some of the data at most of the data or in fact and set it for our training data. And then some of the data will be set aside just for testing. We do want to keep these two dates separate but that being said we can now start to take a look at how to input the data into our project itself. And then how to import the data as a variable so we can begin manipulating it. So the last thing I want to do is just give credit to these guys who've done an excellent job of compiling and composing all of this data into one nice big data set that's easy for us to use. And with that being said let's just switch on back to Python. So here we are back in Python and the first thing we're going to do is just create a new python file so this is just going to be under the domain folder here. And it's going to have a great new python file. This one we can just call something like fraud detection model Now unlike the image recognition one make sure this is a python style by the way will click OK and create that unlike the image detection model that we built. Hopefully you watch that one before this one. We're not going to be separating. The model is sold into a training file and then a testing file and saves the monel like that just because there's not actually much training that we're going to need to be doing. We're actually going to store everything in just this one file so every time we run this we're training and testing it. And I just want to do this to show you both ways of doing things as well. Like I said the output is more geared towards how accurate the model is and how accurately it can detect fraud versus legitimate transactions rather than taking in one specific transaction and are putting fraudulent or legitimate although like I said if you can find that same function that they use to transform the data then that will be you know our model will be able to do that for you. But otherwise we're just going to show you how to seek out the CSP file into your project and then how to store it in a variable. So I have saved my cxxviii file just on my desktop. I'm ok but like I said I think I will have placed us in a folder called resources. Either way the file itself will be called a credit card, does CXXVI and is basically just a CSP file which is kind of like an Excel file if you have used those which is just a big data sheet. And we're just going to simply drag and drop it actually right into the project so just oops. Not really wanting to click. Just make sure you have a selection and just drag and drop it into this folder. It will ask you to move it and you can either copy it or you can actually just move it to actually let's just click. So if you really wanted to you could keep it in that resources folder. Just make sure that when you're providing the path for this file you are providing the path named to the location of the Allsop file. Otherwise it's much easier if you just take it right into the project. Now in order to gain access to this file as well as be able to manipulate it easily I'm going to import panderers. OK and I'll do so as PD and Panas is basically a library that gives us access to a lot of big data set manipulation functions which just make it really easy to take in a file stored in a variable and then perform various manipulations on it such as separating the data into X train y train data as well as a lot of other manipulations so we're just going to store the results in something called a credit card data. Okay. And we're just going to be equal to PD. It's read CXXVI. Nice function. How ready for us and all we need to do if it's imported into the project is going to be to provide the actual CSP file names just credit card dot SVM make sure you do the extension so credit card dot C S V. Now like I said if you wanted to keep it in your resources folder make sure you're providing the actual path name to it. So you know maybe like resources Dasch credit card or C-s feel the effort would be rather than just the name. As I can write just the name because it's already part of the project. So I guess we can just save this and actually run it. Just a quick look at what the data actually looks like Alternatively you can just double click and open this if you have something that reads GSB files ENCEL good. Otherwise we can go to overrun Windows and select the run option and we'll make sure we're running our actual fraud detection model file. Now like I said this is just going to actually going to read. It doesn't have anything to output so we can just print out our credit card data and give it a rerun. And this should just kind of print out all of the stuff.

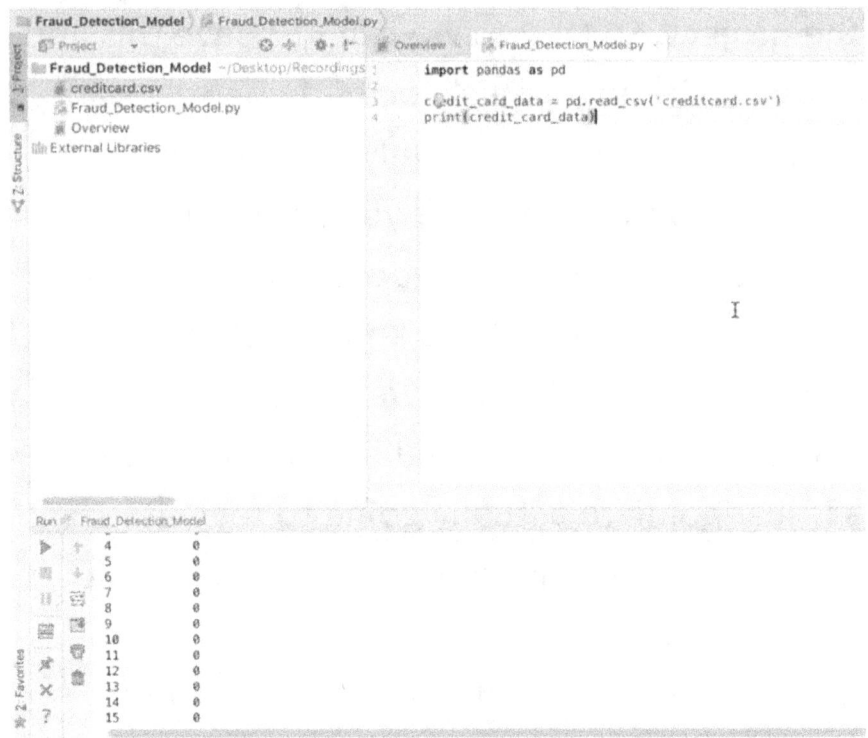

It's probably not going to print every single row and column; it will kind of end up truncating the data as you can see. So it is just going to take a look at this to recognize that we have a First the numbers column Time column and then the features 1 through 28 are where is where it ends up. Yes. And then the amounts. And finally there should be a class as well. And here is the class either 0 1 for each of those transactions. So I would recommend taking a moment just to understand the dates of the LSA mall and I'll explain as we go exactly what each component of the day is doing for us anyway. And our next section will be dealing with actually manipulating this data, separating out the pieces we want and storing them in respect to variables so that we can better build up our model.

BUILDING TRAINING TESTING DATASETS

Hello everyone. This is where we left off in the previous section. We'd learned a little bit more about the dates that we pull into the project here and I've just stored in the variable credit card data. After we ran it and printed everything out it outputs pretty much the whole dataset just truncates it less as you can see with these dots. So if we had to look at it kind of understand what's going on. Expect you to understand what these numbers mean exactly in the columns we through the 28. But just understand at the end of the day these columns the 1 through V 28 are going to be our inputs and the Clauss columns which we scroll down to the boss and we see this clause that has either 0 of the legit ones or ones for these fraudulent transactions. Those are going to be the outputs that we want. So that's actually what we're going to be working on in this section is blissing our big data set into four smaller sets. One is going to be for the X test, one is going to be for the Y test. One will be for the X train and one will be for the white train. Once we have these data sets play support we can Moken actually manipulate them to hopefully eliminate that bias. I talked about earlier in which we know that the data is very heavily favored towards legitimate transactions and that could really screw things up later on but we'll save that for the next section that's just welcome to break out data apart into again the training and the testing data and then into the inputs and outputs. So as you can see I've just added this comment here just as important because that's just what these couple of lines are doing . We can actually get rid of the print statement if we want. And I think this is what I'm going to do at the end of each of the sections we cover all just kind of annotate what we've gone over in the previous section so that when you start up the next section you have all of the previous stuff annotated and you know exactly what those lines of code are doing because especially once you get to the end of the projects and try and look back we don't know what a single line of code is doing then that can really confuse you for the rest of the project. So if you see all these extra comments and stuff that's all I'm doing I just don't think it's very practical to me to spend a lot of time typing these comments out while we're recording. But that being said, let's get to work. So splitting the data up is going to require about six different steps. Some of them will take a little more work than others but to start off we know we're going to need some of our non-prime functions which again give us the ability to manipulate data inside of arrays and big data sets. So it is important for non-pilots to start and all impulses and pay. OK I'm sure you write any code. Let me just make a few quick comments so step number 1. To separate out data is going to be to shuffle or randomize the data so shuffle slash randomize the data. And this will just help to break up any annoying and unwanted clumps. Next step is going to be changing our class data to what's called one halt encoding and explain why we'll need this in a second. Basically it's just a way to input the data into a nicer form into some functions such as a soft Max or the chophouse functions. They like this encoding. OK so step number three is going to be to normalize our data. So if you look at the dataset A lot of the values are negative. Some of them are greater than one. We just want to convert everything into values between 0 and 1. It just makes the data a lot nicer to deal with. OK so step number four is going to be splitting up x and y values. So as I'm sure you know from the previous tutorials X These are typically our inputs and y values are our outputs. So like I said earlier the x values are going to be those columns, the ones through the 28 an hour y values are going to be off-Terra encodings. The outputs are all going to be basically each a matrix of 0 and 1 and I'll explain why after all one Hunton coding. But basically the y value is just going to be whether or not the transaction is fraudulent or legitimate. After this we'll want to actually spell out data into those four sections. But before we can do that we want to convert the data data frame's as they are going to be called up until this point. This is called the data stream. So we're going to convert data frames to non-pay arrays. And this is just going to be a little easier to work with specifically to float those two as well just require one line of code as I enjoy you know tent's afloat does like to work a lot with lotos he turns great on finding number six is going to be the final task. This is just going to be splitting the final data into our next slash y train slash test. And this is just going to be basically the four different sections that have X train and y train and then x tested by test. And this whole process is going to be geared towards placing a day into four sets So let's get started. And again our first step is just going to be to shuffle or randomize our data. So I'm just going to store the results in something called out on a shuffled data and this can just be our current day sesterces stored in credit card data and we're just going to call on this function called sample. We just pulled up a sample here for some reason it's called a sample that just basically shuffles the data. I'm going to answer in one parameter. Track equals 1. So this is just a fraction of the data we're dealing with in this case is just going to be one which means all of the data so we're basically just going to shuffle that all around. So next up is our encoding we can solve this in something called one hot data. And this is just going to be we can call on actually a built-in Panda's function cooled PD dogs get dummies and we'll get dummies in a day frame in this case is going to be our shuffled data. Okay. And it's going to ask for a call that it wants to split into one heart encoding. Well that column if we zoom Mountain take look our data is going to be the clock column. So again we want to convert these into because right now they're in a format like this 0 0 0 actually the wrong kind of comment. See that's 0 for a 1. Well we want to actually convert this to a form that looks a little more like this zero or in the case of it being legitimate in which case it's a zero. Who wants a one and a zero and in the case when it's fraudulent. Well once something like this is 0 and a 1 instead. Like I said this is just going to provide us a best way to fit this into some of our functions a little later on. So we need to specify that we're going to be breaking up our last column. We can do that by calling on columns equals because it might take in multiple columns we'll put this in an array and we'll just pass in the named clause which will again split up this clause column into this format here. Next up step number three is going to be to normalize out data. So again this is just taking everything and breaking it into or converting it to a value between 0 and 1 just feeds Besa into our models. So I'll call this something like normalized data. Okay. And this is going to just require some basic calculation. So we'll take our total data here which in this case is just going to be one hot data minus our one hot day to the minimum. So don't men. And just open a closed bracket say And then we're going to divide this by basically the max minus the men. So one hot day Saddam Max minus one hot day sir. Men Again this just converts it nicely into a format where everything is between 0 and 1. Next up is going to be splicing up our x and y values. I guess I should probably zoom in as it might be kind of hard for some of you to read. If it's you presumed out and as we know our exile is all going to be basically all of those columns be one 3:28 and hour y values are going to be basically just this one hot day a column which in this case is just going to be the class of zero and cost one is that will be cooled once it splits up. So we can do this over two lines but it's easier just to do over one. In fact you know what let's make things a little more readable for you guys let's just do it over two lines. So let's start first with the X data. So let's call this on the circle x. And usually they like the X to be capsulized that's just going to be a normalized data and we want to call this dot drop function which is basically going to take in a column name and it's going to drop all of the data or it's going to keep all of the data and drop just the data in that column. So in this case or do we have it converted our data into one hot data. The cost column is again going to be split into two classes one called Class unschool zero and one class on the school one. So rather than just passing in class like this we have to pass in class zero. And we'll also have a Palsson class on the school one. So I would do if you are unsure about why this is popping up is after each of these stages just kind of comment out the rest of the code and prints how each of these lines so do you shuffled the data prints out the shuffled data after you've combusts everything to one hot data then print that out after you've normalized it. Print that out and keep doing this until you've got a grasp on exactly how each of these manipulations is changing the data that we're dealing with. It's much easier of course to understand what's going on if you can visualize what each of these changes is doing. We're just going to answer in fact one more promise is just going to be access equals one. And then because we have ex-colonies We'll need our wife values also we can just go diea funds school y. This is basically it just can be our normalized data and it's sort of calling that job. We actually do want these in here so we don't drop them, we just get these. So we'll call on out of Ray specific index and the ones we won are just going to be class underscore zero again and class class on the school one. All right. So again could have done these in one line by saying School X comment on school y equals this Colma this. But this is just a little easier to read. Ok so after this we'll want to split the x and y values so we want to convert our data frames with these guys here into our non-pilot those two arrays. They will be simple enough. We can do array underscore X or something and set the sequel to. And we do it as an array in case this is going to be a non-pay array. We want to specify what values we are going to be using in this case are just going to be the values of this particular day of frame so we'll go DPF underscore X Daut values. And we want to specify some kind of encoding. So we'll just go floats 30 two I guess we'll specify data type so D type equals float does. And will do pretty much the same thing for dx on school Y. Let me just show you that syntax I was talking about earlier just in case you've never seen it. So you can go de-funded go y equals and then just add a comma here and then we'll basically just take this copy and paste. And instead of doing the T.F. an X always we want the y values in the same encoding float too. So we'll just be basically loops. I think externally got rid of something the head did. So it's just basically taking what we would have done over two lines here and just testing it all on one long line so I know this is a bit harder to read but it just takes up a few lines of code. All right. And the final step here is going to be splitting up our data into these four sets. So we've already split the data into two sets. We have a little power x values and all of our wife values but we want to go one step further and split probably about 80 percent of these into the training and then the remaining 20 percent can be tested. So actually let's just create a variable that will represent the training ratio. Let's just call this something like train size train size is going to be equal to zero point eight times or 80 percent times the length of Outwood data for the length cost of re unschool X or Y. It doesn't really matter. And at the end of the day we want to make sure this is an end. So I'm actually just going to compass this in brackets and put it in here. So to make sure again it's an integer form. And now we can just use ranges and our upper bound and lower bound to allocate the certain parts of the data that we want into the training and testing data sets. So just because this is going to be hard to see if the rules in Demps going to zoom out now will be cool , I guess we'll call the X and Y values rule X and rule y values. So we'll sort of rule X train. And you know what let's put in tuple level the X train and of rule why should we lower case y train. We don't set the sequel to this tuple here we're going to put in our array x x ray unschool X OK and we'll want a range and then we know we're going to want our RE war II and what to do because I put D.S. with why that's weird.

```
import pandas as pd
import numpy as np

# Import and store dataset
credit_card_data = pd.read_csv('creditcard.csv')
#print(credit_card_data)

# Splitting data into 4 sets
# 1. Shuffle/randomize data
# 2. One-hot encoding
# 3. Normalize
# 4. Splitting up X/y values
# 5. Convert data_frames to numpy arrays (float32)
# 6. Splitting the final data into X/y train/test

shuffled_data = credit_card_data.sample(frac=1)
one_hot_data = pd.get_dummies(shuffled_data, columns=['Class'])
normalized_data = (one_hot_data - one_hot_data.min()) / (one_hot_data.max() - one_hot_data.min())
df_X = normalized_data.drop(['Class_0', 'Class_1'], axis=1)
df_y = normalized_data[['Class_0', 'Class_1']]
ar_X, df_y = np.asarray(df_X.values, dtype='float32'), np.asarray(df_y.values, dtype='float32')
train_size = int(0.8 * len(ar_X))
(raw_X_train, raw_y_train) = (ar_X[], ar_

# 0 -> [1 0]
# 1 -> [0 1]
```

Press ^. to choose the selected (or first) suggestion and insert a dot afterwards ⇥

```
171   0.004455  -0.026561   67.88
68    0.108821   0.104533   10.00
67   -0.002415   0.013649  217.00
```

Sorry this should be a re unschool why K-1 array unschool why a particular range also. So it will go. Basically let me just make this easy to see from zero so nothing on the left hand up until our training size. And then again from zero up until our training size is now still 80 percent of our total data into our X train y train. And then we can do the same test and we test again. If you want to put them all on one line you can all just put on the two lines to make it easier to read. So you know, let's just copy all of this. That was why I zoomed out originally because I actually usually put them on just one line like this and it makes for a really long line but the gnomes make things easy for you guys to read. So this will just be our next test and why test And we're going to go and start from zero to train. So as we go from train size 2 0 0 to the end of the array. And then again from train size up until the end is that you're right. And again this is just allocating the first 80 percent to these guys. Here are the X train y train and then the remaining 20 percent which will be the last 20 percent to X test and by test. And then there's another reason why we shuffle up the data so that we're not guessing any kind of a bias again. And hopefully they'll kind of just randomly distribute all of the ones and zeros. So at this point we have successfully split our data up into our full values, our training and testing the x and y and algae all of those values. Then again if it's unclear any of these steps along the way why we are doing each thing then just kind of print out the end results of each of these so for example if we shuffle the data maybe do something like print shuffle data. After you've taken the one hot date and maybe printed one hot data and so on and so forth. And once you can actually visualize the changes in the data set that makes it a lot clearer as to why we're making these changes. And so that when we come to manipulate the data later on and change up the values into the format we want it will be a lot clearer as to why he would take all these steps and exactly what data we're dealing with when we're dealing with the X train or the white train or the X test or the white test but otherwise because we split the data up we can end this here and move on to the next section which will be manipulating stuff. Again all kind of annotate each of these lines anyway but do check them out for yourself. It will really help to make things easier to understand.

ELIMINATING DATASET BIAS

All right, so we just finished separating our big data set of the credit card data into our four many data sets. About 80 percent of the data is allocated to our X training and white training data sets and then the remaining 20 is allocated to the X test and the Y test. Now despite some kind of transformations we've done we're still left with the issue that our data is very very heavily biased towards legitimate transactions. So this is a big problem when we're trying to train our model because our model is obviously going to see a lot more legit transactions. And so when it comes time to test the validity of the model it's more likely to say that a transaction is legitimate versus Brauchli even though it might be fraudulent just because that's what it's being more exposed to that's what has had more time to learn about. So what we need to do is devise a clever way to basically make our model take more notice of the fraudulent transactions and that will hopefully help to eliminate the bias at least a little bit. Now this will be done through a process called logic racing and is actually quite a simple process and very practical. We'll get back to that in a second. I just want to take a moment to ask Prince exactly what kind of ratio we're dealing with so that hopefully you guys will gain a better understanding of the gravity of the issue. So you can follow along if you want or you can just watch me write these few lines of code just basically just going to be printing out the ratio of Trojan versus legitimate data and I just hit the run window which is why things might look like I'd look a little different from before. So I'm just going to create a couple of quick variables I'll do like a count SRL not do logic first and then a count fraud. And that's just going to be a Pido unique which will get all the unique elements of an array. The array is just going to be our original credit card data. I'm not going to take any of the modified data sets. And I'm looking for the column Clauss. As this is going to be the main way in which we're going to be able to tell if a transaction is legit versus fraud. Remember it has this for the one point encoding a value of 1 in the cost column and fraud. Legitimates have a value of zero and fraudulent have a value of 1. OK so we also want to return counts. I'm going to set that to be true and we are looking for the index ones so this will separate basically our will legit transactions and so will those that have the value zero and 0 strode into those half the value of 1. Okay. Next still needs some kind of a ratio so I can actually print out the percent. So I'm just going to call this fraud ratio. Okay. And this is basically just going to be our count fraud. Okay. Divided by the total amount of data. So count the Jets plus count fraud. And I can convert this I guess I'll convert the since with floats. So just wrap this whole thing in a float and then at the end I'm just going to print this out. I'm going to print something legitimate you know I'll say something like. Percent of fraudulent transactions. And I'll also add in the actual fraud ratio here. So if I were to now go ahead and run this. This is just going to print out some very small percentage that represents the number of fraudulent transactions versus the number of legitimate transactions. So as you can see this is actually the percent. So this means this is basically points 1 7 2 percent of transactions that offer fraud. So this means that about 99 percent of all of the transactions that the model will be exposed to as of now will be legitimate. So you can see that model is very heavily favored. The legitimate transactions I mean think about if you were tasked with telling the difference between two objects and you basically only saw one type of the object and almost none of the other type of the objects. At that point it's very difficult to tell that the other object might be indeed different from the first one. However if we placed great importance on objects too even though we might have seen the last few times it would be a lot clearer in our mind as it will have a higher way saying it will stand out a little more.

```python
# 6. Splitting the final data into X/y train/test

# Shuffle and randomize data
shuffled_data = credit_card_data.sample(frac=1)
# Change Class column into Class_0 ([1 0] for legit data) and Class_1 ([0 1] for fraudulent data)
one_hot_data = pd.get_dummies(shuffled_data, columns=['Class'])
# Change all values into numbers between 0 and 1
normalized_data = (one_hot_data - one_hot_data.min()) / (one_hot_data.max() - one_hot_data.min())
# Store just columns V1 through V28 in df_X and columns Class_0 and Class_1 in df_y
df_X = normalized_data.drop(['Class_0', 'Class_1'], axis=1)
df_y = normalized_data[['Class_0', 'Class_1']]
# Convert both data_frames into np arrays of float32
ar_X, ar_y = np.asarray(df_X.values, dtype='float32'), np.asarray(df_y.values, dtype='float32')
# Allocate first 80% of data into training data and remaining 20% into testing data
train_size = int(0.8 * len(ar_X))
(raw_X_train, raw_y_train) = (ar_X[:train_size], ar_y[:train_size])
(raw_X_test, raw_y_test) = (ar_X[train_size:], ar_y[train_size:])

count_legit, count_fraud = np.unique(credit_card_data['Class'], return_counts=True)[1]
fraud_ratio = float(count_fraud / (count_legit + count_fraud))
print('Percent of fraudulent transactions: ', fraud_ratio)

weighting = 1 / fraud_ratio
raw_y_train[:, 1] = raw_y_train[:, 1] * weighting
```

So it would be a little more likely to recognize it. And that's the whole idea behind this logic wasting is that instead of just having like a 1 and a zero as we did with these one hot encoding tenses we're going to multiply these by a certain amount and that will introduce what's called a higher waiting to fraudulent data. So for example let's say that before this logic waiting I have just the one zero for legitimate data and then the zero one for fraudulent data on the logit waiting. I might have let's say I multiplied by some constant 10 or something. Most days would have a wait of 0 and 10 instead of 1 and 0. So then because this is a high number or a higher weighting will pay a lot more attention to it when it's being trained so that it's more likely to look out for those numbers when it's actually being tested. So as for the actual constant We're going to be multiplying by I think I'll go with one over this fraudulent ratio. So basically one divided by points 1 7 2 and I was going to see the results in some variable here and I'll literally just call this a waiting. So racing is going to be basically one divided by our will throw wood ratio. So maybe it is a good idea that you actually take a moment to type the stuff out although you don't have to print if you don't want to. And this should give us a number I think of over 500 might be closer to 600. I think it's like five hundred and seventy something and we'll basically multiply all of our worldwide training data by that value so that any time it sees a 0 and 1 it's going to multiply that one by. In this case about 507 something just the way the sync number is. We don't however want to multiply our legitimate data or also defeat the entire purpose of applying a heavy away saying to our fraudulent data. This is a very common technique used for very unbalanced data sets. Obviously it's much better to deal with a balanced set in this case just due to the nature of having a lot more legitimate transactions and fraudulent transactions in general. It's kind of hard to get around without resorting to this technique. So we're basically going to have to get out of your way on the train. And now we're going to reassign it and actually will need specific parts of it. So we'll need basically all of it but we're only interested in the ones where basically any time it'll see a one in the right hand column which again indicates fraudulent transaction. What we're just going to set the scene to why a train will pass. And again the same thing. And we're going to multiply this by Alwa wasting. So that actually takes care of the issue pretty much for us. And that's just about all we really need to do to hopefully eliminate the bias; it's not going to eliminate the bike completely. But again because this is going to be quite high on Mono we'll pay a lot closer attention to the fraudulent transactions than to the legitimate ones when it comes time to actually train and recognize what is fraud and what is legit. So just a very quick summary before we move on and actually start building our model because Audi says have heavily biased was legit transactions we have to apply a weighting using a technique called logic racing to our fraudulent data. And basically we just got the ratio of fraud to legit. It spits out this very small number. We're just applying a wasting of one divided by that so it sets it to a large number and then we're most playing any time we see of petroleum transactions of 0 1 instead of 1 0 in our one hot encoded data and with multiplying that by waiting so that we're going to well apply a heavier casing to Roselyn data as the model pay closer attention. So without being done that's pretty much all of the day set manipulation we need to perform and so we're ready to start building up our actual testing model or training model I suppose. So this will be done over a few different sections as I don't want to kind of overload you guys with too much information at once as always. You know, keep annotating things at the end of each section. I'll add some comments here. You can see a bunch of comments about the stuff we did in the last section and so we'll continue to do so.

BUILDING COMPUTATIONAL GRAPH

Pay everyone with the application of our long waiting. We've hopefully eliminated or at least minimize the bias between the legitimate and the fraudulent data. And we have our big data set that separates it into these for many day sets. And so now I think it's time to start actually building up our computational model starting with the construction of the actual graphs itself. So this is basically going to be a few layers off several different kinds of tens of flow nodes and is going to be quite a bit more complex than the simple linear regression model we built in our tens of flow intro. Now because it's going to be quite a bit more complex the reason being that this is a much more complex issue to deal with than what we had dealt with previously. We're going to be building this over a few sections but the underlying principles remain the same. We're going to have some kind of input in this case we'll actually have a few layers rather than just one. Will have some kind of an output. And the idea here is to count up the loss and to minimize that loss over several different epochs. If all of these words are completely unfamiliar to you then I'd really recommend you watch our introductory 10 slow tutorial just so that you are not completely lost in the next sections. And as always I'm going to annotate everything at the end of each section and I'll try to go a little more slowly and separate things out so that you have a break between each of the different sections. But otherwise let's get started with an important four tenths of flow of course. So we want the importance of flow. I'm just going to label it as t. So we gain access to all of the tensile flow functionality by the way, just minimizing the run window here just to give ourselves a bit more room as we are kind of running out of space getting a bit closer now. So the first thing we need to do or while we might want to do is just to define a few constants that we're going to use throughout. So it will need some kind of an input dimension and some kind of an output dimension. So we'll say the input dimensions are really cool at that. All going to be the shape of our input array in this case. It's going to be basically the C units that are in our X train data set so I know the X train dates that contain many many different rows but it only has about 30 columns. The V-1 to feed 28 plus there's a time and an amount column we'll want those as well. So we went instead of the row x train. What are you going to use the array unschool X which is just before the actual allocation of the training and the testing data. Although to be honest it probably doesn't really matter anyway. But we'll go. And actually no we don't want any. We want our actual array itself and we'll go dark shape and we once index one. So this will now be basically an input about a tensor of 30 elements so that we can input any one of the flow ex trains or the rule X test as we feel is necessary. So the training data, testing data and the output dimensions themselves will just be two units wide because we are going to be outputting that one and zero value that we saw here with the hot encoding. So we're just going to set the actual output dimensions mentioned equal to the same as our ray unschool Y shape. And again we want one from the next. I'm going to add a couple more variables. I might not necessarily understand why we use these numbers yet but just bear with me here. This is basically just going to be specifying the number of cells we want in each file layer. So we know the input layer is going to be just the 30 cells the output dimensions are just going to be the two cells. And then in each of the middle two layers we all can have 100. And then about 150 cells. So I'm just going to call this variable something like Nahm. Les one cell spells that wrong. K Adam is going to say that the sequel to 100 will go on layer cells. We're going to set this equal to 150. OK so with these Dali's we're going to now create some actual input tenses themselves. So these are going to be basically placeholder type nodes. So we'll call this something like X unschool or train node. And there's going to be a TFT placeholder and we basically want the placeholder to be the input dimension shape as we are going to be because it's the X train that is going to be taking in some kind of input. So we want these to be left off float to again once the actual tensor stuff so we're going to have this nonne by input dimensions. So about 30 columns here. And I think I'll give this a name as well. Just going to set a name equal to how about let's just call it X train. And we're going to do a very similar thing for our input or our Y train. So he's going to copy that and paste it this time instead of the exchange being by train. And again a similar thing except for our impot dimensions we honestly don't want it to be those units wide. We only want it to be two. So it's just going to take an output dimension as a set of inputs. So output dimensions. And we definitely want to change the name as well. So just going to call it white train. So these are basically going to be these nodes that are going to be used for training so that when we go to run our actual session we're going to need Palsson values for our X and Y train nodes. And I'm sure you guessed that we're probably going to end up using our rule X train an hour of rule by train data sets for these. Now because we've created our X and Y train nodes we need to create some X and Y test nodes and these we can actually just allocate to be constants because we have our actual testing data set here. Rural access an hour rule White says if you want a pulse and different values. I'd recommend you either create placeholders or some kind of variable nodes and then you can assign the value at a later time. Also if you want to test cases one by one then again you'll definitely want some placeholder nodes instead so that you can input values at runtime but otherwise we're just going to set an X test node. And so going to be a similar thing except instead of placeholders just going to be a Constans will pass in the value of our rule X test. Make sure the X test or anything else to get this name off. Let's see we had X train so let's just give it the name of X on a school test and we'll do pretty much the same thing with the Y. So just copy and paste this Y test node concept we want to take in the rule Y test data. And again name to test. Now this is where things get a little weird. I'm going to zoom out so we can hopefully see the bigger picture as kind of hard to see when everything is zoomed in. But we'll basically be building up our other layers next.

```python
df_y = normalized_data[['Class_0', 'Class_1']]
# Convert both data_frames into np arrays of float32
ar_X, ar_y = np.asarray(df_X.values, dtype='float32'), np.asarray(df_y.values, dtype='float32')
# Allocate first 80% of data into training data and remaining 20% into testing data
train_size = int(0.8 * len(ar_X))
(raw_X_train, raw_y_train) = (ar_X[:train_size], ar_y[:train_size])
(raw_X_test, raw_y_test) = (ar_X[train_size:], ar_y[train_size:])

# Gets a percent of fraud vs legit transactions (0.0017% of transactions are fraudulent)
count_legit, count_fraud = np.unique(credit_card_data['Class'], return_counts=True)[1]
fraud_ratio = float(count_fraud / (count_legit + count_fraud))
print('Percent of fraudulent transactions: ', fraud_ratio)

# Applies a logit weighting of 578 (1/0.0017) to fraudulent transactions to cause model to pay more attention to them
weighting = 1 / fraud_ratio
raw_y_train[:, 1] = raw_y_train[:, 1] * weighting

import tensorflow as tf

input_dimensions = ar_X.shape[1]
output_dimensions = ar_y.shape[1]
num_layer_1_cells = 100
num_layer_2_cells = 150

X_train_node = tf.placeholder(tf.float32, [None, input_dimensions], name='X_train')
y_train_node = tf.placeholder(tf.float32, [None, output_dimensions], name='y_train')

X_test_node = tf.constant(raw_X_test, name='X_test')
y_test_node = tf.constant(raw_y_test, name='y_test')

weight_1_node = tf.Variable(tf.zeros([input_dimensions, num_layer_1_cells]), name='weight_1')
biases_1_node = tf.Variable(tf.zeros([num_layer_1_cells]), name='biases_1')

weight_2_node = tf.Variable(tf.zeros([num_layer_1_cells, num_layer_2_cells]), name='weight_2')
biases_2_node = tf.Variable(tf.zeros([num_layer_2_cells]), name='biases_2')

weight_3_node = tf.Variable(tf.zeros([num_layer_2_cells, output_dimensions]), name='weight_3')
biases_3_node = tf.Variable(tf.zeros([output_dimensions]), name='biases_3')
```

So these can be thought of as being the inputs into a model. And now we need to build up one gate. None of these cells lay it to. And then finally our outputs an output layer which will kind of take on this dimension to reach these layers we're going to need the weight of the as well as the biases of the laya. And each of these I'm going to set two variables because the values will be changing as we're trying to optimize the loss. So here goes lay a one I'm just going to call the first one. Wait for one node. And is going to be asked this time is going to be a variable remember Castle V and we'll basically start our variable node with an array or matrix of zeros. So actually L2 TS dot zeros caseless are basically going to be a matrix of zeros. We have to specify the dimensions in this case which is how the input dimensions first. And then we want our number of lays of 1 cell so they are 1 cell. And I'm just going to give this a name. Probably best to where possible give these guys a name so you can identify them by name rather than just relying on this variable. So in this case ocal this something like Waite's one OK and that's that's all we need to do for the weight one note here. So at the end it looks kind of like this and this is why it zoomed out. Just because I can't really fit everything in this zoomed in window so it's just a variable note. We're basically setting up a matrix of zeros. This is going to be in this case about 30 by 100 I believe. Yep that's right. And the name is just wait one. Now when these create biases one too much. So it's just going to call this bias one note and this is going to be another variable so TFT variable node. We will start up an array again this time TFT zeros also but instead of this matrix we're just going to have it be a single dimension array and the array is just going to be our what number of late one cells and we'll give it a name as well so name just call them something like Pisces 1. Now it leads to a very very similar thing to this in our Lay is two and three. And again I'm not expecting you to understand exactly what's going on right now. As I said, all kinds of annotate things as I go at the end and everything all comes together and we'll be a lot clearer towards the end once we can see the big picture here. So I'm actually just going to copy this paste and paste and we're going to modify these so this will be two and two and there will be three and three outputs whatever you want. It's up to you. So in this case instead of input dimensions and the number like a one cell stretch you can have a number of one cell and the numbers lay it two cells and then we're going to do the two downa will give these different names this is going to wait for in Pisces too. Jim's going to change names right now. These three locate and then similarly We're going to do a number of later two cells. And then this one is going to be just our output dimensions. And the node Bice's Node 3 is going to be output dimensions here and just make sure the names are Okan to match. So hopefully you can kind of see what's going on here. We're basically having the inputs and our number layer 1 cells and on the Byass is matching this. Okay. And then we're having the number of Layer 1 cells by number two cells and then of course number two cells. And then we have numbers two cells an output and then output here. So every line is just kind of connecting together here. So except for the outputs which will just be its own kind of separate thing. We can almost think about these as being the output of one layer is kind of the inputs of another layer. So that's why Crace of the constants are top rather than just feeding in actual values because if for whatever reason I decide that my model's not good I want just the number of cells then I can basically just change these numbers here without having to change everything. Now each of these variables because right now there's just basically matrices of zeros and we don't want them to be heroes. I mean that's not very useful to us. Our goal is again to create some kind of a loss. We use a different last function number four. We're trying to optimize that loss by adjusting the values that all of these have. That's why there are variable nodes instead of the constant noise. But you're going to be our actual test cases and the placeholder nodes will assign values at natural runtime. Now again finding out exactly how many layers we want in this case we have three. And the number of cells in each layer is a bit of a bit of an art and can take a lot of trial and error. Also it's purely dependent on the task we're trying to achieve. We are doing just a very simple linear regression. It was easy to accomplish with just one layer of cells. In this case retching doing something a lot more complex working with a much much larger dataset. So we're going to need to go a few layers deep and as always as I said right at the beginning and are probably rehashed lots of different times. This isn't the only way of doing things. It's just one of many different ways we can build up a model like this. But otherwise our graph is well on its way to being built. So we're going to want to start building up our actual training and testing functions and a nice way to start to optimize the amount of loss or rather minimize that loss by creating some kind of loss function. Minimizer and a bunch of other functions. So basically the graph is almost constructed. Now we have all the components necessary but we need some functions to actually bring everything together and to call upon once we're running everything. So that's what we're going to do in this section coming up. We're just going to be working on building those functions. We might take a couple of sections depending on how long it's going to take but otherwise I'll take what I did here and just be sure to review and understand what's going on at least kind of roughly before we move on to the next sections.

BUILDING FUNCTIONS TO CONNECT GRAPH

We have some inputs for our training. We have some inputs for our testing as well as we have a few layers built up. So the first layer actually could have taken the input from the user that we're going to pulse. The second layer then goes through the third layer and by the time it finishes the third layer it will actually output some kind of a tensor which will be able to tell us whether or not the transaction is fraudulent. Of course we'd have to run this through for every transaction but we're not going to do that just yet. We'll save the actual testing and training and testing portion for one or two sections from now. What we'll do in this section is add in a few functions that will help to regulate the flow of information through these three layers. So we'll start off by creating a function that will take in some kind of attention and input. It will run that tenso through these three layers and then it will return another tensor which will be kind of the result of several different machine learning functions. And this just kind of helps us to fit the data after we've done that we can add it and stuff like a way to optimize the amount of loss that will need for the last function and then an optimizer and then we'll add one or two other little bits and pieces. So let's start by creating that networking function. And you know what I think I'm actually literally just going to call this network game because that's kind of what it's doing it's running our inputs through this neural network. So it's going to take in an input tensor. And this could be for example our trains training nodes or our testing nodes. Either way this is going to be a nice way to kind of predict our output should be. So we'll have to run it through three different layers. We'll start off by crazing the first layer with some kind of a function. And this is going to take our input tensest going to multiply it by a bunch of stuff and output something. OK then we'll use whatever output so lay a one as an input into it to do the same thing or probably use different functions than the output layer to be fed into three. And then the output of the last three is what our function is going to return. So we'll sort of with a of one and we're going to use some turns of flow functions so TFT and is that tends to load on neural networks and we don't start off with a sigmoid function. Now there's a few different functions we could use. I chose sigmoid because it is a good function that fits the data well. It's kind of hard to see what function we should choose that provides the best fit without an actual graphic visualization of the data. So if there's some way you can take that CXXVI data sheet and actually cross it or perhaps the modified data. The stuff up here the rule y train were extraneous stuff. If you can find a way to actually grasp that and that fits a line through it you'll see that sigmoid is a good function to actually do this providing a well facing line. So this will basically be the results of some matrix multiplication so we'll call on a TS dot map malfunction or matrix multiplication for short. OK and we want to multiply our input tensor by the weights of one node which is the first layer. So we'll do the comma here. It's one node and this is just going to multiply these together. And then of course we want our biases. So plus biccies one node. And that's actually all we need to do for laya one. Now we'll actually do a pretty similar thing for our next couple of days. Except that instead of taking in the input tens or multiply not by the corresponding weight so two or three Larche take the results off layer one layer one itself and then multiply that by weight to node and then in the last three we'll take it to and multiply that by weight 3 node. But for the next day we're actually going to do something slightly different. We're going to use what's called a dropout function and this helps prevent our models from becoming lazy. So this is kind of a weird concept in that if the model is right too many times then it kind of becomes lazy because it thinks you know I've been right this many times I'm going to be right in the future. So with the troppo function this helps to cause the actual model to keep paying attention to the data it's given. So we'll set it to equal two. We'll start off with T.F. And again and again and then sort of sigmoid we'll do a chop out And then within the drop out we'll do another sigmoid function and then we'll add the actual kind of decimal that will or the decimal number that will represent the amount of drop we want to add. So we'll do a TFT and sigmoid. Okay. And in the sigmoid we want to again use our matrix multiplication. So we'll do T.F. towards that mall again. And instead of the importance tensor course we want layer 1 and we want to multiply it by our weights to node. And then of course we want to add the bias's plus piracies to nodes. And then also because we're still inside our Europos function we need to specify exactly how much dropout we want. If we set this too high then it's going to cause our model to become precessing to low cost models or become slow. But we set it too high then you know we might as well add in the dropout. I think a point eight five is a pretty good number to choose because you can kind of modify this if all models are super and accurate but this is kind of this is the number I found to work well. So that's our second layer complete. Now we want our third layer which is going to be the final output layer. So we'll have layer 3. Okay. So to speak to TFT N-N and now we're going to use yet another function. And this one is going to be a soft max function. Now we're using soft Max because this soft my function works really well with one heart encoding. And if you remember the outputs are going to be in that one whole encoding format. So there is going to be a 1 0 or 0 1 or in case it's actually going to be 1 0 or a zero and five hundred and seventy eight or something like that. Whatever the results of the awakening was and I guess that this just really works well with that kind of encoding. But otherwise we'll follow a very similar format so Ts dot matrix multiplication again we want the results of late to escape and we want to multiply it by our weight three nodes plus our biases three nodes. Okay. And then at the very end we want to return our last three so we can just return layer 3 so at this point we have this function that can basically take in some kind of impot tensest. This could for example be the trading data or the testing data and it will make some kind of prediction based on what it thinks it thinks should be the actual results by running it through these layers and then we'll compare the predicted values to the actual values we output. And this will help us to calculate the amount of loss. And then of course we want to try to optimize the loss by minimizing it. So let's just make up a couple of prediction and prediction variables for both our white test and our white training data. So we'll just call this something like white train production OK and I'm going to stop my train prediction equal to the results of the network . The input tensor is just going to be our next training node. So X train node OK and we'll do the same for testing. But obviously it's going to be why test prediction can't be done and we're going to set the sequel to the results of the network and we'll impose our X Sheppey X test node. OK so now we have some kind of way to predict what we think we should output by running everything through this networking function. Now what we want to do is calculate the amount of loss which is basically going to be comparing the actual output to the predicted outputs. So this is actually going to be slightly different. The last function is what we used in the intro to tenths to flow. This is going to be a soft Max last function simply because we're dealing with again one home coding soft Mikes that work so well with that. So the loss is in our case cooled cross entropy and just makes more sense given what our next step will be. And we go and set this equal to its losses. Okay. And we're going to go with that soft Max cross entropy again. We don't want the soft sophomore's cross entropy, we just want this regular one. Now we're basically trying to compare how we're predicting to the actual output. So remember to keep in mind the are x train and y train nodes not the testing ones because Constans the X train and y train nodes are just placeholders. So although this won't necessarily contain a value yet when we go to actually run our session we will input the value. And so all of these placeholders will take home values, all the variables will be changing and so on and so forth. So we want to enter our Y train node and our Y train prediction loops in this and train node. We want the prediction and are still choosing the wrong one that should be our train prediction that we go okay OK so again this is just going to be some kind of a last function. So now that we have the last function we want an optimizer which is going to be used to minimize this loss function and is going to be using that same gradient descent. So I'm just going to call this optimizer so optimizer is going to be equal to this. T asked Doc to train dots and we're going to use what's called an atom optimizer function. So just one of many different optimize it kind of functions. Again I'm just showing you one way of doing things. Like you said there's lots of ways of going about doing this out of optimization is just the one I went with and it still works on the principle of gradient descent. So we need to put what's called a learning rate in here. And in this case we wanted to learn slowly because as you can see here it recommends point 001 much. You are going to up this a bit and go with a point 0 0 5. And we're trying to minimize our cross entropies so don't minimize cross entropy so essentially what this is is a gradient descent function it's learning is going to be put 0 5 so that's by how much it'll change each of the values and is going to change the values in such a way to minimize our cross-bench of which is our loss. And this is based on the difference between the actual outputs, the white tray node and the predicted outputs. Now the last thing I want to do before we go over everything is just kind of rehash what we've covered. It's going to be to create a function that will actually predict the accuracy of our output. OK so I'm just going to call this something like predict or calculate accuracy Okay. And this is going to take in an actual amount. So actual as well as a predicted amount and then this again just going to compare the actual value that we get that we output versus the predicted value that we want. So we're just going to convert these both into indices so we're just going to say actual is equal to p dot org Max and we get in the indices of our actual am going to go with one and that will say the predicted is is going to be and again and P-Dog Max this time will enter and predicted and we will have one. And then at the end of this we just want to return basically the comparison of these times 100 so we can get some kind of an actual percent rather than a decimal number. So it will just take some toll. And then we went and Peto had equal weight and that's just about right and would take in our actual and our predictions in this case. I think it's actually going to want these in the opposite order. So we'll do predicted and then actual. Okay. And then we're going to divide this by our predicted shape at the index 0 and we also want to multiply everything in here by 100. So I'm just going to say 100. Multiply it by all of this and that's just going to be a nice way to actually calculate the accuracy of our final results. Okay so now we have a few functions to actually run everything through our network and come up with some kind of a prediction versus the actual values. We have a way to find out what the loss is and how to optimize that loss. And then the way to finally calculate the accuracy so all that remains now is to devise a way probably some kind of a function to actually run our session and then feed in some training data and then see what gets outputs then we can compare the accuracy of what is outputted versus what we think should be outputted but that's what we're going to save for the next section or next two sections. Okay. So in this section we started off by crossing our networking function which just basically takes in some input. It runs it through each of our three layers by taking the output of the previous layer and using that as an input. We used a few functions that just fit with data and nicely to do so. But at the very end it's going to return the output which is just going to be kind of that one has encoded data.

```python
# Third layer takes in input from 2nd layer and outputs [1 0] or [0 1]
weight_3_node = tf.Variable(tf.zeros([num_layer_2_cells, output_dimens
biases_3_node = tf.Variable(tf.zeros([output_dimensions]), name='biase

def network(input_tensor):
    layer1 = tf.nn.sigmoid(tf.matmul(input_tensor, weight_1_node) + bi
    layer2 = tf.nn.dropout(tf.nn.sigmoid(tf.matmul(layer1, weight_2_no
    layer3 = tf.nn.softmax(tf.matmul(layer2, weight_3_node) + biases_3
    return layer3

y_train_prediction = network(X_train_node)
y_test_prediction = network(X_test_node)

cross_entropy = tf.losses.softmax_cross_entropy(y_train_node, y_train_

optimizer = tf.train.AdamOptimizer(0.005).minimize(cross_entropy)

def calculate_accuracy(actual, predicted):
    actual = np.argmax(actual, 1)
    predicted = np.argmax(predicted, 1)
    return (100 * np.sum(np.equal(predicted, actual)) / predicted.shap
```

We use this to predict our white training and our white testing data using the predicted values versus the actual output values and these we don't know yet because we haven't in Pisin anything so will remember these are just placeholder notes up here. So we have a way to calculate the last will have to run that through of course of the session and then way to optimize that loss by having a learning rate of point 0 0 5. Trying to minimize the actual loss across entropy and then a way to again just calculate the accuracy by entering the actual value that outputs adv. what we predict should outpace it. So once again I'm going to say these so that hopefully will clear up any kind of confusion. Are there any easy steps along the way which you got lost? Definitely go back and watch us again. It's important that you understand what's going on here so that when we go to actually start training and testing our model you do know what's going on. But otherwise once you're good all again I'll tell you everything at the beginning so that at the beginning of the next section you'll have these nice comments. I'll tell you what's going on. But otherwise let's get to actually training our model.

TESTING THE MODEL

So we just finished building up a way to train our model and we did this in this statement. So now let's build a way to actually test the accuracy. So hopefully you guys did run it through and as you can see the last also about 1.4 and ended up about Point 8 too so we know that the model is improving over time. I'm sure given more Polk's if we did like what was in the parks I mean that would take a long time to do. If we did I'm sure this loss would decrease even further. Now this is really the benefit of training models more and more the more we expose it to data and the longer we give it to change then obviously it's going to become better with time. But in the interest of saving a bit of time I'm not going to train a thousand times or even more if you want to go ahead and do that then feel free to do so but I'm just going to finish off by showing you how to test out your model so we can kind of see what the end result is and how accurate the models finally going to be. So we're going to write a little bit more code within this statement. And then after that we can write some extra code to test specifically the reward detection accuracy. Now when we're printing out the current accuracy model what do we include in this if statements that we're printing out a new accuracy with each iteration. This will be slightly more beneficial to us as we'll be able to see how the accuracy of the model will change as well as the loss minimized. So the way we're going to assess the final accuracy of our model is by comparing our way. Why do we see where it is up here? It's our wide test node which is a constant and that's going to be the constant outputs against the wide wide test prediction that's going to be this one which is basically going to be the results of passing that train's data through this network. Now if you remember passing this data through the network as it's being trained will change its variable values. So whereas our white test showed up here is a constant. The predicted node will be variable. So this difference between the two is going to determine how accurate our model is. So assuming that you want to print a printout the accuracy every 10 pulk or if you just want to print out the end that's fine just be sure to exclude outside of the statements and actually outside of this for loop as well. But otherwise you'll basically want to evaluate what's current value. Each of these nodes hold so we want to evaluate our why test no. That's this one up here as well as our work y prediction Y test prediction. So we are in the Y test node and will basically have the same value before and after training. It's a way of prediction that will be changing as we improve the actual accuracy of the model. So I'm just going to call this something like Final Y test and this is going to be equal to the results of our Y test note Dalt Evo.

Okay. So just going to evaluate what value we test now holds. And then we're going to save the final y test prediction. And this is going to be equal to why underscore test prediction is not evil. So basically the same thing but obviously apply to our why prediction. And I think I spelt that wrong prediction Yep definitely mix those around. So now with the help of our accuracy function which we built up before we can actually just Palsson the actual value versus the predicted value. And then we can use this to test how accurate the model is going to be. So let's just call this result something like Final accuracy and there's going to be results of pulsing into our correctly accuracy function. First the actual values of the final y test. Okay. And then the predicted values to the final y test prediction. So this is going to output some numbers, probably going to be a float. And we want to print this out again off to every 10 pulk once more if you do want to print all the stuff out just once at the very end. Be sure to exclude the outside of this for loop. So just pass it on this indentation here. Okay. But otherwise we're just going to again format some kind of a print statement. We're going to print something like Curran's accuracy and then we're going to again format this. I think I'll go to either 2 or 4 decimal places. Doesn't really matter, it's entirely up to us. Oko to add two decimal places because I want a percent. So a point is asked and then a half a percent. And then we want to do the Tulls format and we want the answer in our final accuracy. Now that being said we can successfully test the accuracy of the overall data set. But if we want to print out the accuracy of just throw a detection model. So basically the accuracy which it detects is just fraudulent cases. We're going to have that right just a little bit of extra code and it's going to look very similar to this but will be slightly different as we're going to have to access not allow our entire final test data set but just the final way test data sets where we're dealing with a one on the right hand side. So this final strong specific detection stuff I'm just going to put this actually outside of the with statement and I will find a way testin how predictions will hold their values even once we exit this. Okay. And just doing this for the sake of a little bit of variety. Now I'm going to stay zoomed out when I type this because if I do zoom in and we get some of the lines of code being cut out of the window. So OK zoom in and focus on each part towards the end but otherwise I'm going to call this something like Final reward Y test. Cape and they will have a final thought by prediction. So we'll actually use the same results now we calculate it up here. So we'll just enter in our final test that's going to be the final results. But we just want the stuff on the right hand side. So I'm going to use some kind of weird syntax actually. Let me just zoom in for this specific part. So in the index. We're going to put our well against the final y test and then we're going to choose an index from this. We're going to choose specifically the right hand side. So she should insert the comma there. And then I'm going to say it equals one. And yet this might look like some pretty weird notation. But basically this is just going to say that we're only interested in what's on the right hand side of this. And we're only interested in when that right hand side equals one. OK so kind of confusing syntax but that's all it's doing is it's just selecting the right hand side when the right hand side equals one as if you know if you remember from Malwa one encoding the fraudulent cases will look a little like this. OK so the right hand side will be one. And that's what we're testing for here and all this is actually saying not to for obviously because we're defining it inside of our if statement here. So I'm just going to actually do this exact same thing outside of the IF statements that we get a final final reading. So let's just end this here. We're going to paste it here. So this is still within our statements. And actually this stuff should be outside of our four loops of the hills zoo mountain let me just close up this run window it's like this. We're going to shift tabel shift back so we are once outside of this for loop but still within the with statement. So those statements are different in that any variables defined within it are not restricted to just being available within here. So in this case I'm just changing to final accuracy and this way we get kind of the constantly updated accuracy and then the very final accuracy output. So now we once again do this and then we want the same for the prediction. So we're going to go to our final fraud test and then we'll go on score prediction. Okay. And this is now going to be equal to again our final test but we want the predictions to be just going to capias and we want the index but we still want the index specified hayah. So I'm just going to copy this here and paste it in here. So now that we have the test and the way to test prediction, what we need to do is run it through our calculate accuracy function once again. So we're going to say final roared accuracy is going to be equal to calculate accuracy. We need to pass on our actual sort of final fraud. We test it out of the sky. And then I will sign on for a world wide test prediction. And in the end we can print the results out so it prints something along the lines of. Final reward specific accuracy. And then again the format I mean just means tests and we'll do the format here and we can do this to two decimal places again just because we're dealing with another percent. Support 2 percent and then in the format we want our final fraud accuracy here final thought accuracy. So we go. All right. So at this point we are actually ready to run the model. We will be training and testing at the same time. So even though you've already trained at once because we didn't save that trained model we'll just train again. So when we actually go to start training at our pools and then pools of recording rather than come back to it once we have finished training and then testing. But basically what we're doing here is within the with statement but outside of the for loop I just basically copied and pasted this and just changed this word here and we're getting the final evaluation for the test. And the prediction note and then calculating that final accuracy that would have been calculated right in that we're printing that out. And then outside of the with statement we're testing the fraud specific accuracy so this is taking both fraudulent and legitimate cases into account. This is just testing the fraud specific cases and the accuracy at which our model detects those. So we'll probably get two pretty different figures. Now this will likely be a lot more accurate than this again just due to the fact that our data set has been exposed to a lot more illegitimate transactions than fraudulent transactions as well. Our test case contains a lot more legitimate transactions as well than fraudulent transactions. So you know there is still going to be that bias even though we helped to eliminate it slightly. Using that logic way of saying. But with that being said let's give this a run sir. Hopefully there are no errors that really shouldn't be but I'm going to pause the recording as soon as we see the first e pop pop up. And then again resume once I get the final tallies printed out and then I'll kind of wrap things up there. So there we go. Current accuracy Pt. 1 5 and so pause here. Let it run and come back to you guys. And we're back. OK so the model has finished training again. As you can see we're kind of getting better and better with each accuracy restarts of précis decimals. This is Point 1 5 percent terrible accuracy obviously. And as we got as we went on we kind of jumped a bit and then made a huge jump up here 288. And finally we ended up with about ninety nine point three nine percent overall accuracy. So this means that it will be able to source legitimate from fraudulent transactions with close to 100 percent accuracy. Let's just call this 99 percent. However detecting the rewards specific stuff so completely negates all of the legitimate transactions and just recognizes fraudulent transactions. Unfortunately we were only about eighty two point five six school this AC3 just to be a little optimistic. So again this slightly lower accuracy percent could be due to a few different factors one being that the data again was very heavily biased towards legitimate transactions two being that even the testing data was again quite biased wasn't just that transactions didn't get exposed to as many fraudulent transactions as possible. And there may be either the learning rate was a bit too low or even a bit too high and maybe we haven't trained at quite long enough. I'm sure if we were to run this again a thousand 10000 you know 100000 e pocks then this current loss would decrease and we'll be able to detect even higher accuracies but otherwise that is pretty much it for the basics of building a fraud detection model least with credit card fraud. Now like I said I'm sure this is just one of many many different ways that we can go about building this model. Perhaps if we added more layers it would become a less accurate Pep's if we use a different number of cells for each of the layers again it could be more accurate and less accurate. So kind of playing around these parameters does take a little bit of work and not quite guessing and checking but a similar sort of concept is needed to kind of optimize your model. You just need to play around the premises a little bit and see what works, see what's improve your model was not improving your model and then work towards obviously improving things. Some models if you tailor them commercially can achieve pretty much 99 percent accuracy or higher across all boards. But of course that would help if we had less access to a little more data otherwise. With that being said and our model completed I'll just kind of run through things with you from start to finish in the order in which we implemented everything. So we also, if just kind of eggless, are most familiar with the data that we had about the dates of about 284 thousand transactions, something like that again only a little less than 500 of them were legitimate and the rest were legitimate. So there is a heavy bias to deal with now the data itself was separated into a few parts we had features v 1 through V 28 which was just basically a bunch of features of the transaction itself that all transactions themselves that were converted into numerical inputs. So this may honestly be the hardest thing about building up this model is getting access to that data and then using the correct function to turn the actual feature of the transaction into numerical data. But once you can do that. And we already have some dates set to do that for us that are kind of taken care of. Then we worked on sorting our data into these four sets. We first shuffle that convert into that one whole and coding normalize the dates to make it between 0 and 1 separates it out x and y values. Remember the X was a feature v 1 through the 28 and the Y was just that one on encoding of class 0 and Class 1 of this converted it to an array of floats. And then basically separated out our training and testing data. The first 80 percent of the data was allocated to training and the remaining 20 percent was for testing. After this we figured out a way to basically print out our ratio. We got basically points 1 7 percent were fraudulent and the rest were legitimate. So we had to kind of try to balance that back out with what's called longship rate logic wasting. So it basically multiplied all of the fraudulent transactions by this number about 500 and 78 or 1 divided by point 0 0 1 7 to make our model pay closer attention to the fraudulent transactions. So with a higher weighting our model will recognize the frozen transactions more and we'll kind of pay closer attention to them just because this wasting is so much higher than the regular one. Although as we can see it wasn't quite as accurate and wasn't 100 percent effective, we have a lower final accuracy for the SRODES specific stuff. But I mean no model is perfect and can always be tweaked and improved in a way after this. We worked on actually building up our computation of cross using a bunch of tens of functions just to specify some constants up here number Salz and the first and second layer is the input dimensions are going to be those x rays. Also about the features V1 survie 28 plus stuff like the time in the mounts. And then the output was just going to be the two cells which I guess this one has just gone to be the two cells for that one Harton coding. We created some notes here the placeholder for our X and Y train, some constant Strout x and y tests and then about three layers in our total neural network so one was for the input then we passed it to the second. And finally the third Witchell output again either that 0 or 1. Next we define a few functions to first help us parse everything through the layers. This was our network function. We have just a bunch of other functions such as a chop out and a sigmoid and then a soft Max and these are kind of helps fit a line through our data so that we can work on minimizing the loss. Next we came up with some prediction variables. These were what we would predict. Without training our models so these or other these are the values that we would have altered towards the end whereas the actual test up here is the constants these X and Y tests these were the actual should be outputted kind of values. Next we defined a cross entropy variable. This is to measure the amount of loss. This is what we're trying to minimize using our optimizer. We just chose an atom optimizer here and this last function was just to compute the accuracy at the very end. And then finally in the last couple of sections we built not the way to actually train our model. And so I need to test it with training at basically 100 times running the data through our model 100 times using the rule X train and the rule y train data which we modified at the very beginning came up with this new cross-bench preschool with each IPAC and then every 10 people which just kind of printing out the time the current iPad and the current lost value as well as towards the end the current accuracy of our model. So we saw that drastically improved over time as well as the cross-bench yourself lowering which is exactly what you'd want. Then at the end once our model was fully trained so took the for loop after running 100 times we're printing out the very final accuracy recording that we are based on our final values in the Y test node on the Y prediction node as well as the third towards specific values. So this is just the overall accuracy of the overall data so legitimate and fraud. How good is our model for sourcing legitimate versus fraudulent stuff? Whereas the fraud specific accuracy's just focusing on how well it detects fraud versus fraud and legitimate. All right, so there you have it, a complete fraud detection model. Like I said there's always a lot of room for improvement. It's just one of many different ways we can build this. Some possible things you might want to try out or maybe modifying boastful the number of cells that we're adding to each layer so you could try modifying these values here. I wouldn't recommend modifying the input or the output because those values should stay the same but maybe try playing around with these values, try Grace values less values less than these and so on and so forth. Another way to May be improved or it might actually be a detriment to your model would be to apply a slightly different weighting so a higher waist because it's a little more attention to the fraudulent data whereas I wouldn't recommend going any this or Also model won't recognize the old stuff as well other ways we could modify it would be to maybe add a fourth layer. So between our input and the output I'd like to lay a two point five I guess or I guess make that new layer layer 3 and output layer upon layer 4. Although this being said if we're trying to make our model too complex it's just going to be it's just gonna take a really long time to run and to train. So in our case this works pretty well but doesn't hurt to try things. Another way we can change up the model is to change the specific functions we're using. So we're using a sigmoid rather than a dropdown sigmoid on a soft Max. I would recommend finishing up with a soft Max just to the one in coding and in our case I think the sigmoid probably fits the data a little better.

```python
    actual = np.argmax(actual, 1)
    predicted = np.argmax(predicted, 1)
    return (100 * np.sum(np.equal(predicted, actual)) / predicted.shape[0])

num_epochs = 100

import time

with tf.Session() as session:
    tf.global_variables_initializer().run()
    for epoch in range(num_epochs):

        start_time = time.time()

        _, cross_entropy_score = session.run([optimizer, cross_entropy],
                                             feed_dict={X_train_node: raw_X_train, y_train_node: raw_y_train})

        if epoch % 10 == 0:
            timer = time.time() - start_time

            print('Epoch: {}'.format(epoch), 'Current loss: {0:.4f}'.format(cross_entropy_score),
                  'Elapsed time: {0:.2f} seconds'.format(timer))

            final_y_test = y_test_node.eval()
            final_y_test_prediction = y_test_prediction.eval()
            final_accuracy = calculate_accuracy(final_y_test, final_y_test_prediction)
            print("Current accuracy: {0:.2f}%".format(final_accuracy))

    final_y_test = y_test_node.eval()
    final_y_test_prediction = y_test_prediction.eval()
    final_accuracy = calculate_accuracy(final_y_test, final_y_test_prediction)
    print("Final accuracy: {0:.2f}%".format(final_accuracy))

final_fraud_y_test = final_y_test[final_y_test[:, 1] == 1]
final_fraud_y_test_prediction = final_y_test_prediction[final_y_test[:, 1] == 1]
final_fraud_accuracy = calculate_accuracy(final_fraud_y_test, final_fraud_y_test_prediction)
print('Final fraud specific accuracy: {0:.2f}%'.format(final_fraud_accuracy))
```

But you know there's a few different functions that we can try out. Maybe using a different function would produce a different output. And then finally the stuff we've been over before may be different. Optimizing it altogether would produce different results. Obviously, different learning rates would help people model learning faster or slower. And the number of parks and a higher number of sleepwalks will make your model more accurate but will also take longer to train and to test. But with that being said I'll leave you guys to kind of play around with things a little bit on your own. We have lots of other machine learning models and tutorials to build. So once you are comfortable with this we can move on to some of those. So be sure to check out the other models.

www.ingramcontent.com/pod-product-compliance
Lightning Source LLC
Chambersburg PA
CBHW052138220526
45471CB00004B/1433